KALEIDOSCOPE

SWANSEA

Edited by Simon Harwin

First published in Great Britain in 1999 by
POETRY NOW YOUNG WRITERS
Remus House, Coltsfoot Drive,
Woodston,
Peterborough, PE2 9JX
Telephone (01733) 890066

All Rights Reserved

Copyright Contributors 1998

HB ISBN 0 75430 373 X
SB ISBN 0 75430 374 8

FOREWORD

This year, the Poetry Now Young Writers' Kaleidoscope competition proudly presents the best poetic contributions from over 32,000 up-and-coming writers nationwide.

Successful in continuing our aim of promoting writing and creativity in children, each regional anthology displays the inventive and original writing talents of 11-18 year old poets. Imaginative, thoughtful, often humorous, *Kaleidoscope Swansea* provides a captivating insight into the issues and opinions important to today's young generation.

The task of editing inevitably proved challenging, but was nevertheless enjoyable thanks to the quality of entries received. The thought, effort and hard work put into each poem impressed and inspired us all. We hope you are as pleased as we are with the final result and that you continue to enjoy *Kaleidoscope Swansea* for years to come.

Contents

Gowerton Comprehensive School
        Maggie Elsey   1

Mynyddbach Comprehensive School
Amanda Palmer	1
Carla Thomas	2
Claire Buckney	3
Michelle Demery	4
Claire Hughes	4
Donna Clements	5
Jayne Nicholas	5
Kate Davies	6
Lucy Davies	6
Victoria Bevan	7
Vicky Allen	7
Carli Derrick	8
Amanda Jackson	8
Amy Mainwaring	9
Natasha Wilson	10
Gemma Jones	10
Toni Thomas	11
Melissa Phillips	12
Kelly Dean	12
Suzanne-Louise Ward	13
Kirsty Wilshere	14
Marie Barry	15
Victoria Davies	16
Leanne Brown	17
Samantha Lewis	18
Stacey Williams	19
Jodi Hanton	20
Laura Bujega	21
Kerry-Anne Nash	22
Samantha Davies	23

Pontarddulais Comprehensive School

Danyal Williams	23
Kate Elizabeth Glass	24
Ali Saad	25
James Frazer	26
Amy Davies	27
Natalie Adams	28
Bethan Turner	29
Aaron Shingler	30
Annie Lee	30
Jordana Thomas	31
Emma Roberts	31
Tom Williams	32
Robyn Lee Shefford	33
Adrian Hire	34
Emily Chatfield	35
Dylan Lewis	36
Sam Richards	37
Sarah Richards	38
Nicola Ann Lewis	38
Kelly Richards	39
Eva Manning-Davies	40
Elisabeth James	41
Rhian Harris	42
Samantha Lewis	42
Lewis Baker	43
Adam Rogers	44
Emma Buckley	45
Rob Nagi	46
Keith Phillips	47
Jonathan Harris	48
Siân Gray	49
Siân Cliff	50
Michelle Huggleston	51
Kylie Hearne	52
Louise Williams	53
Katrina Grant	54
Ashley Lewis	54

Sharon Louise Jones	55
Ruth Taylor	56
Joanne Leddy	57
Jason Elvins	58
Nicola Davidson	58
Daniel Hennah	59
Chris Watkins	60
Carl Mainwaring	60
Stephen Liddiard	61
Rhian Williams	62
Rachael Stephens	62
Penny Davies	63
Simon Pearce	64
Catherine Gwenter	64
Liam Coleman	65
Wendi James	66
Mark Corcoran	67
Samantha Rees	68
Tabitha Ford	68
Sarah Brown	69
Leyah Hillman	70
Matthew Brooks	70
Michael Cooper	71
Daniel Jones	72
Robert Courtney	73
Adrian Paton	74
Jason Lee Cole	74
Kelly Mainwaring	75
Nicholas Morgan	76
Karen Lewis	76
Stephen Howells	77
Charlotte Whalen	77
Sarah Treviso	78
Steven Card	78
Catherine Stilwell	79
Fay Mogford	80
Vicki Erasmus	80
James Rogers	81

Angharad Evans	82
Elaine Speyer	83
Victoria Davies	84
Stephanie Dew	84
Craig Cox	85
Adele Boobier	85
Sean Owens	86
Jack Matthews	87
Nathan Evans	88
Sadie Thomas	89
Nathan Raddenbury	90
Fallon Kift	90
Emma Black	91
Kayleigh Watkins	92
Nerys Clement	93
Matthew Sibley	94
Nicola Hearne	94
Oliver Richards	95
Angela Brugnoli	96
Jenna Edwards	96
Rebecca Collins	97
Kieran Downing	98
Elinor Lewis	99
Maryanne Temblett	100
Jonathan Eynon	100
Kirsty Howells	101
Sarah Carruthers	101
Hannah Simpson	102
Kathryn Thomas	102
Siobhan Shannon	103
Michael Williams	104
Kelly Stilwell	104
Emma Bolt	105
Kirsty Wilson	106
Richard Thomas Masurier	107
Sarah Westron	108
Emma Thomas	109
Tom Bradshaw	110

Nia Jermin	111
Julie Anthony	112
Rachel Williams	113
Robert Barnes	114
Sara Lloyd	115
Emily Dawson	116
Lee Harris	116
Mathew Fuge	117
Dario Fisher	118
Thomas Millard	119
Aimee Richards	120
Michael Thomas	121
Jasmine Kelly	122
Alan Evans	123
Cheryl Scott	124
Jenna Griffiths	125
Luke Raddenbury	126
Stewart Edwards	127
Gemma Coffey	128
Laura Kaltenbach	129
Dale Thomas	130
Kirsty Evans	131
Joanne Richards	132
Amber Carlisle	133
James Mainwaring	134
Leon Thyer	135
Simone Morris	136
Kaity Lee	137
Amanda Robertson	138
Linda Taylor	139
Michael Evans	140
Alexandra Hawken	141
Anna Nowak	142
Charlene Smith	142
Sarah Price	143
Gemma Evans	144
Gemma Roberts	145
Sarah Worthing	146

Vanessa Moyes	147
Caroline Jones	148
Sarah Gwenter	149
Daniel Carlisle	150
Vaughan O'Neill	151
Beverley Taylor	152
Faye Chatfield	153
Stacie Ellison	154
Sarah Whitehead	155
Gabrielle Thomas	156
Louise David	157
Ceri Gazey	158
Daniel Kelly	158
David Borthwick	159
Rhian Arrowsmith	160
Rebecca Chapman	161
Samantha Mogford	162
William Bootyman	163
James Beynon	164
Scott Thomas	165
Philip Mathias	166
Alistair H Veck	167
Steven Harrison Dewitt	168
Sarah Evans	169
Cheryl Davies	170
Emma Caie	171
James Lockwood	172
Alex Whitehead	173
James Rogers	174
Carys James	175
Jack Joseph	176
Lino Davies	177
Leanne Lloyd	178
David Gower	179
Kali-Ann Joseph	180
Rachel Buckley	181
Sarah Probert	182

Ysgol Gyfun Gwyr

Rhian Horlock	183
Owain Gimblett	184
Zöe Rasmussen	184
Angharad Jones	185
Gemma Waters	185
Lara Bragger	186
Ffion Davies	186
Ian Davies	187
Laura Beveridge	188
James Owen	188
Angharad Roberts	189
Nia M Seaton	189
Gwenllian Thomas	190
Kelly Griffiths	191
Lisa Marie De Benedictis	192
Ffion Davies	193
Rhiannon Pace	194
Ceri-Llian James	195
Curon Wyn	196
Carys Jenkins	196
Bethan Edwards	197
Elizabeth Jones	197
Bethan Way	198
Natalie Saunders	198
Christian Densley	199
Elinor L Jenkins	199
Catrin Morgan	200
Rhys Padarn	200
Andráea Parker	201
Christopher Huw Davies	202
Rhys Jones	202
Alice Loft	203
Sara Moran	204
Lisa M Evans	204
Amy Williams	205
Rhian John	206
Rebekah Smitham	206

Rhianwen Davies	207
Verity Jones	208
Rachel Anderson	208
Trystan Rice	209
Sarrah Morgan	210
Holly Davies	211
Cari Griffiths	211
Rhian Ivey	212
Rhiannon Morgan	213
Rhian Nurse	213
Bethan Reddy	214
Rhiannon Reddy	214
Iestyn Austin	215
Mari Jones	216
Carys Pope	216
Abigail Ede	217
Siân Eleri Jones	218
Leigh Alexandra Woolford	219
Samantha Swain	220
Carys Rees	220
Sara Griffiths	221
Suzannah Smyth	221
Iwan Palmer	222
Kelly Hall	222
Grace Morgan	223
Sarah Daniel	223
Gwyneth Thomas	224
Sophie C Dark	224
Hannah Morgan	225
Megan Davies	225
Amy Evans	226
Angharad Jenkins	226
Sarah Aggus	227
Rachael Gregory	228
Rhys ap Gwent	228
Tyla Williams	229
Alun Rhys Chivers	230
Carys Humphreys	231

Rhys Cullen	232
Sara Elinor Tuckey	233
Nerys Thomas	234
Robin Jones	235

Ysgol Gyfun Ystalyfera

Hannah Barrow	236
Jonathan Davies	237
Gwenllian Richards	238
Emma Morgan	239
Ceri Wyn Lodwig	240
Leighton Howells	240
Richard Brett Oliver Mallinson	241
Caroline Louise Ashill	241
Clementine Hollister	242
Mari Alwena Jones	242
Owain Bates	243
Andrea Bazley	244
Cadi Dewi	244
Elen Hâf Richards	245
Kim Richards	246
Bethan Morgan	246
Hywel Rees	247
Angharad Carys Thomas	248
Fiona Michelle Humphreys	248
Rhian Indeg Snowdon	249
Emily Fyfield	250
Matthew Maddocks	250
David Roland Parker	251
Roxanne Guard	252
Craig Robert Fisher	252
Daniel Briggs	253
Nia Rhianwen Williams	254
Lowri Williams	255
Gareth Thomas	256
Catrin Reed	257
Angharad Jones	258
Roxanne Chinchen	259

Stephanie Hawcutt	260
Lydia Davies	261
Isla Sheree Humphreys	262
Owain John	263
Hannah Gange	264
Katie Grounds	265
Bethan Wallace	266
Frances Dennis	267
Rhian Bazley	268
Jessica Wearing Evans	269

The Poems

STEPHEN

Even though you're gone,
You will always be with me,
Always in heart,
Always in thought,
Even though we had some
good times,
You will never leave my mind.
We will meet again someday
Maybe in heaven,
Never in hell,
I did not know it would
be this hard,
It went so quick,
And yet so slow,
Even though you're not here
You will never leave me!

Maggie Elsey (11)
Gowerton Comprehensive School

FEELINGS

You are the most precious
Rose in the garden,
The most delicate in the field
Yesterday I felt happy,
Now I feel unhappy
Because someone picked you.

Amanda Palmer (14)
Mynyddbach Comprehensive School

CHILDHOOD MEMORIES

Fresh and crisp as the morning air,
My new school uniform.
A white polo shirt and a grey pinafore,
A blue jumper to keep me warm as the sun.

My new black shoes glistened like dew,
My bag, all clean, held my crisps.
Mummy did my hair in bunches,
I looked like Pippy Long-Stockings!

As we walked to school, the clouds departed,
Like people from an airport.
The sky was thunder-like; misty and grey.
I thought it was going to rain.

We reached the school gates, I pushed them open,
Cautiously, like a flower opening its petals.
The building was bustling with children,
I grabbed Mummy's hand.

A tall, thin lady, waved to me,
My eyes were waterwells, filling up.
My lips trembled,
Then raindrop sized tears poured down my face.

I took off my coat,
Hung it up on the hook.
Mummy kissed me on the cheek,
Then waved like the teacher had.

My lead heavy hand waved back,
I stumbled into line.
I was trapped in another world.
We all entered the classroom, we were silent, like mice.

All day I talked and played with new friends,
Happy, I was a circus clown.
After break, we had milk and apples,
Before the giant-size teacher read us a story.

Then it was time to go home . . .

Mummy came and put on my coat.
My smile was the size of an ocean!
Swinging my bag, I left.
I was a kangaroo all the way home, skipping and hopping.

I couldn't wait to go back,
The next day,
To see all my friends again.

That was my first day at school.

Carla Thomas (14)
Mynyddbach Comprehensive School

YOUR IDOL

Doesn't everyone have an idol?
Someone they love and respect,
Someone they could look to,
In trouble and in fret.

They might be an author,
They might be a star,
They might be someone you worship from afar.

No one can pick your idol,
No one can tell you that's wrong,
If you believe in someone,
Then you can follow them strong.

Your idol might be your parents,
Your idol might be your pet,
Your idol might be anyone,
Anyone you respect.

Claire Buckney (12)
Mynyddbach Comprehensive School

MY FEELINGS

Today I feel frustrated
Today I have detention
I have it after school
for a whole hour.

I am not looking
forward to it
I don't know what to write
so I feel very angry

And I am in school
and tired too
I want to go home now
and not to detention.

Michelle Demery (14)
Mynyddbach Comprehensive School

SILENCE THAT SCARES

As I walked down that strange and spooky lane,
Out popped silence and brought me pain.
Instead of wolves howling and dogs barking,
I heard nothing, not even cars parking.

It was then that I realised it was silence that scares,
That followed me home, even up my stairs.
Under my bed I heard a spooky thing,
When all of a sudden a ghost started to sing.

There I was, lying in my bed,
Letting my imagination run wild in my head.

Claire Hughes (12)
Mynyddbach Comprehensive School

FEELING

Love is happy,
Hate is sad
When someone loves you
You are happy.
When someone hates you
You are very sad.

Happy is when you laugh
Sad is when you cry
Happy is excited
Sad is depressing.

Life is not always happy
Life is not always sad
But together they make up me!

I'm happy some days
Sad the next day
I'm happy when I am with
My friend
I am sad when I am in school.

Donna Clements (14)
Mynyddbach Comprehensive School

GOLD

Gold is for the stars
on a starry night
looking for the shooting stars
down under the
moonlight.

Jayne Nicholas (13)
Mynyddbach Comprehensive School

WITCH GRAN

My name is Sarah,
My gran is a witch,
I told her a secret once,
She grassed me up, the snitch.
I went to visit her one day,
She nearly turned my hair dark grey.
She wanted me to join her,
But I said I'd rather grow fur,
I told her that, so she turned me into a cat,
She turned me back in the end,
But I still have this weird bend.
My brother Fred is now a frog,
He hides inside gran's hair,
Her hair is all matted,
And torn and tatted,
Which makes the perfect lair.
She uses all sorts of spells,
And potions with some disgusting smells.
All she lacks, as far as I know,
Is a broomstick, to get up and go.

Kate Davies (12)
Mynyddbach Comprehensive School

COLOUR

C olour reminds me of poetry
O range is bright like the sun
L over is red on Valentine's day
O range feels like I've got to pay
U mbrella reminds me of rain
R ed is blood when you're in pain.

Lucy Davies (13)
Mynyddbach Comprehensive School

MARY

Mary is a nutter
Mary is a witch
Mary dresses funny
Mary makes me itch

Mary speaks to lampposts
Mary talks to trees
Mary rants and raves at things,
That you and I don't see

Mary lives in a little flat
All upon her own
If you listen hard enough
You can hear her groan.

Victoria Bevan (14)
Mynyddbach Comprehensive School

COLOURS

The colour red is for romance,
The colour orange makes me dance,
Yellow is the colour of corn,
Grey is depressing and makes me moan,
Purple can make me happy and bright,
But then again so can white,
Rich people like the colour gold,
Silver makes me feel brave and bold,
Jealousy is the colour green,
In the night black can't be seen,
But my favourite colour is nice light blue,
We've all got favourite colours me and you.

Vicky Allen (13)
Mynyddbach Comprehensive School

THIS IS HOW I FELT!

This is how I felt,
This is how I felt,
When I sat my exams,
I was nervous,
I was scared,
I was worried.

This is how I felt,
This is how I felt,
When I met the boy of my dreams,
I was in love,
I was in a dream,
I was so happy.

This is how I felt,
This is how I felt,
When I lost my dog,
I was lost,
I was lonely,
I was so upset.

Carli Derrick (12)
Mynyddbach Comprehensive School

POETRY IN COLOUR

S ummer is hot and nice
E ven the cats are playing
A utumn is cold and nasty
S pring is refreshing
O n a cold winter's night
N ovember one month until Christmas - Hooray!

Amanda Jackson (13)
Mynyddbach Comprehensive School

A Good Night Out

The weekend's here, Friday's the time,
My telephone is like a hot line
I've waited for weeks for this night to arrive.
I'm going to be in the bath by five

Amy, Victoria, Joanne and me,
Are going to town to party
We'll go for a drink in one or two pubs
Then for a dance in one of the nightclubs

The bath has already been run
I'm going to town to have some fun
My curlers have been placed in my hair
Decisions, decisions about what to wear

I bought a black suit the other day
Or my skirt and top will be okay
I've telephoned the girls to check the date
We decided to meet in town at eight

My make-up is done and it looks just right
I don't want to look as if I've been in a fight
My mum says 'Don't be late'
I'll be okay, I'm with my mates

I'm really excited about this night
My mum says 'Don't get involved in the fights'
We dance all night, until we drop
Dance to the music we hear on 'Top of the Pops'

Girls' night out is so great
I end up coming home late
We all go home best of friends
I wish this night would never end.

Amy Mainwaring (13)
Mynyddbach Comprehensive School

COLOURS

There are colours in flowers,
There are colours in bees,
There are colours all over,
The skies and seas.

There are colours in birds,
There are colours in trees,
There are colours in everything
Even a key.

The whole world's colours
It's really great fun
For me and you
It's just number one.

Natasha Wilson (13)
Mynyddbach Comprehensive School

ROMANCE IN COLOUR

Red means love,
Love means romance,
As he takes my hand,
And leads me to dance.

I think of white, then I think of snow,
I think of it as a blanket,
With a little soft glow.

When I think of silver
I think of stars in the sky,
And I think of the little twinkle
That you see in some people's eyes.

Gemma Jones (13)
Mynyddbach Comprehensive School

DUCKO

'Ducko', a sad old man all alone,
carried a bag with a bottle in it,
Stopping dead as he walks,
just to fill up his dirty old cup,
taking a sip from it to give some relief
Then continuing his worthless, cruel journey once again,
Desperately needing a drink to fight back the unbearable pain.

Some people laugh, while others pity
As he stands in the middle of the road
and bursts into an angry rage
Shouting and swearing about any old thing,
He shouldn't be like that, not a man of his age.

He has made up some chants about himself,
Loudly and violently he shouts them all out,
To the young, the old
just anyone who is about
His language is disgusting, as are his gestures.
I don't think he chose to live like this,
Maybe he didn't have a choice.

He used to be a family man,
A loving, caring husband and father.
He knew what it was like to be loved,
and what it meant,
I think he feels bitter for what he once had,
Wishing he could go back to his nice normal life.

But *'No* not Ducko,' says his upset, confused wife,
That is why I feel sorry for Ducko and his sad wasted life.

Toni Thomas (15)
Mynyddbach Comprehensive School

WHAT IS THE SEA?

The sea is the salty water
Which covers the Earth's surface,
It is the monstrous villain
Smashing against the rocks.

Wild winds howl across the ocean
Like predators after their prey,
Flashes of lightning, lights up the sky
Like fireworks on display.

Fiercesome waves twist and turn
As though they were dancing with the wind,
The sea is the salty water
Which covers the Earth's surface.

Melissa Phillips (14)
Mynyddbach Comprehensive School

A SPECIAL DAY

Postman called around today,
With cards to say happy birthday,
Friends will come with gifts and stay,
To share my treats and play all day.
Blazing candles on the cake,
Count the number that they make.
Blow them out!
Make a wish!
Then eat the trifle in the dish,
Soon my friends will leave, well fed,
And time for me to go to bed.

Kelly Dean (13)
Mynyddbach Comprehensive School

MY GRAN

I spent every day with her,
Really lovin' she was,
Until one day,
I'll never forget,
She sadly passed away.

We shared all her sweets together,
And told each other jokes,
She used to tell me all her stories,
Of all the nice old blokes.

Sadly my gran was bed-ridden,
I knew she couldn't walk,
But instead,
Every day,
We used to stay and talk.

I miss my gran,
I really do,
I always wished she's stay,
Or better still,
I really wish,
She'd never gone away.

Suzanne-Louise Ward (13)
Mynyddbach Comprehensive School

SEA MOODS

The sea is a soft blanket of blue,
A calm sparkling dream,
A refreshing tumbling wave,

Then, the rain pours,
the tiger roars,
and scratches at the rocks with
its fierce claws

When it settles down again,
The sea becomes lame,
the tiger is tired and tame,

Sharply comes a crashing storm
The waves like a rhino with its
piercing horn,
charging at the rocks, erupting
Almost like the world being reborn.

The rhino now breaks down to a
Steady roar, exhausted.
The beautiful blue sea, retires
Till morn.

Kirsty Wilshere (15)
Mynyddbach Comprehensive School

THE TRAMP

Sitting in a cardboard box,
eating people's rubbish,
staring with his only eye,
he limps around the street.

Children call him names like 'freak'
the adults call him weird,
he chases children down the street,
waving his stick - a water pipe.

He sits quietly in the field,
reading last month's paper,
singing quietly like a croaky frog,
and plays with Tiger, his kitten.

When night creeps around,
he climbs into his box,
and covers up with paper,
he is peaceful for now.

Morning comes too quickly,
and so do the village children,
I bet he dreams beautiful dreams -
waking up is his nightmare.

Marie Barry (14)
Mynyddbach Comprehensive School

CHILDHOOD MEMORIES

There are still memories for me to treasure
Of love beyond all measure.
Thinking of what I did when I was young
and how I had so much fun.

How I'd played all day through,
or was that only when I was two?
Did I dream about horses while lying in bed?
When having nightmares did I squeeze my teddy bear?

Did I start school when I was three?
oh yes, I fell and cut my knee.
Did it bleed like a waterfall?
Or was it a graze that was so, so small.

I remember my grandad when he was young.
Tall, dark, shy and very handsome.
In photos he was very tall.
So tell me why he is getting small?

I shared his sweets, we laughed and laughed.
When I got dirty he'd run me a bubble bath.
I'm very proud I'm very glad.
To have had him for my grandad.

Victoria Davies (14)
Mynyddbach Comprehensive School

A GOOD NIGHT OUT

It's going to be a good night out
Without a doubt
Tonight's going to be the best
Better than all the rest
Getting ready for this night is a rush
Oh my God, I can't find the brush
I can't do my hair
What shall I wear?
Pink, blue or green -
aquamarine?
I'm going with family and friends
The fun never ends
My parents are going mad
But because I'm allowed to go I'm glad
Waiting in the queue is such a wait
I'm lucky I didn't faint
I finally got in
I threw all the sweet wrappers in the bin
I danced all night
I had such a fright
The bouncers were shouting
I was pouting
It was such a terrible night.

Leanne Brown (13)
Mynyddbach Comprehensive School

A Good Night Out

Oh no!
Only one hour to go
My hair is a mess
I can't find my dress
But it's worth the hassle.

I'm out the door
I'm ready to go
I'm off to meet my friend
I hope the night never ends.

The queue is long
The bouncers look strong
I look different to everyone else,
But I'm only being myself.

We are finally allowed in
It's time to begin
The night is still young
I'm having some fun.

I've danced all night
I have not stopped
My legs have gone weak
Now it's time to go home and sleep.

Samantha Lewis (13)
Mynyddbach Comprehensive School

ANDRE

Walking through the 'Rec'
Alone and afraid.
He hums to himself,
Unaware of the world around him.

His unusual accent drifts around the children.
The youngsters stop and stare at the crazy man
Slowly but steadily creeping towards them.
Ready to abuse him for the third time that day.

His dark curly hair is neatly placed,
His pale face shows concern.
The day's events devour his mind,
He carries on all the same.

Andre has good intentions,
He cares for everyone but himself.
Alone in his large house
The overcrowded emptiness keeps him company.

His smart clothes are expensive,
Although he walks like a poor man
Moving as fast as he can,
Trying to escape from something?

I can't see why they terrorise him,
The polite, young man with good looks.
He's only a few years older than me,
How can he want to break free of his life?

Stacey Williams (14)
Mynyddbach Comprehensive School

MY GRANDAD

My grandad has a joyful soul,
and his heart is made of gold.
I love to see him, because I need him,
and because I love him.

My grandad has always been
a helpful man,
and that is how he got
my gran.

They stick together through
thick and thin,
That's because their love is
from within.

They have lived together for
45 years,
that's how they get on
each other's nerves.

My grandad's skin is soft
and mild,
It's like his personality
from inside.

I hope he'll always be
there for me,
Because I'll always
be there for him.

Jodi Hanton (13)
Mynyddbach Comprehensive School

NUTTER

Like the dinosaurs, he is ancient,
Like a beanpole, he is tall.
'Nutter' they call 'Oi nutter'
The children in my street.

The oddball in our midst
A strange creature.
The village mockery; a target for taunts.

'Old dull Raymond is a loner.
He always has been.
He always will be'
That's what my mother says.

'Old dull Raymond is a nutter'
That's what the children say about him.
I used to think he was a nutter too!

People say he's mad.
Some of them say he's shy.
I just think he's insecure,
Afraid of the deafening silence.

I look at the strange man, in the street
and also at his long white pole.
My heart is a city of pity.

Raymond isn't a loner.
He just spends time on his own.
After all, what about those teddies?
He talks to them . . .

Laura Bujega (14)
Mynyddbach Comprehensive School

WEIRD AND WILD

A strange character I know has the name 'Ducko',
He walks around all day,
Wearing a dirty and stained blue duffel coat,
Sometimes he walks for hours,
Sometimes he walks for days,
Only stopping in the midday sun,
To have a swig of ale.

He makes a home of a bus shelter,
He turns a tatty box into his bed,
Sometimes he does stupid things;
Starting fights or breaking into cars,
Just so he can spend one cold and lonely night,
In a cell he doesn't have to share with others.

When someone sees him they move him on,
As if he was a sour apple spoiling a sweet apple tart,
People don't seem to realise he's human after all,
I guess he'll walk on and on,
Until his days are over,
Never knowing what life he could have led or had.

His life is empty,
He has no friends or family,
Nobody gave him the penny he needed,
To make a pound, so that his life would be complete,
Instead they left him walk the streets alone,
Children just torment him,
Copying what he says or calling him rude names.

To us he's just a star in the sky,
Or a fish in the sea,
There's no need to worry about something there's
A million of,
But one day he'll be like the dinosaurs - Ducko will be extinct!

Kerry-Anne Nash (15)
Mynyddbach Comprehensive School

A Good Night Out

I went to a disco,
With my friends,
Dressed up
With my hair curled to the ends.

My high heeled shoes,
And my lipstick dark,
My rosy red cheeks,
The same as my friend, Sophie Cooze.

It wasn't very good,
I covered
My hair with my hood,
I was not in the mood.

I went home with my dad
I was late - Mum was mad!
My stomach was really bad
I felt ill!

Samantha Davies (13)
Mynyddbach Comprehensive School

Who Is She?

She's pretty!
She's sweet!
She makes me feel warm!
And at home!
She also cuddles me
like a teddy bear!
Who is she!
She's my mum!

Danyal Williams (11)
Pontarddulais Comprehensive School

SEASONS

The babbling brook
Makes rushing sounds
Clear blue skies
Not a cloud in sight
Swallows flying high above
Sun shining on the river nearby
Reminds me of diamonds and crystals

Bluebells of May sway in the sun
Fresh, green grass pierced with dewdrops
Blooming buds blossom on the trees
Like an artist giving the final touch to the canvas
With a hint of paint
The hills of a small country village
The valley down below waiting . . .
The parish bells ring.

Reds and yellows
Golden brown
Scatter among the slippery floor
The wind picks up
Howling through the trees
Umbrellas high overhead
Dripping with rain
The startling moon hangs high above
Another end to another overcast day.

The lake frozen over
White snowflakes fall down silently
No leaves on the trees
Children playing in he snow

Quiet crisp town
Cold air gives you a chill
When you go home
Warm by the burning fire
Putting up the Christmas tree
Before we know
Spring is here once again.

Kate Elizabeth Glass (13)
Pontarddulais Comprehensive School

I NEED THIS I NEED THAT

I could see myself skating in those cool skates
Elegant, smooth and fast
So sharp, royal red the best of the rest
'Oh yes,' but
I got no bucks no lucks no pocket money blues

I could just feel those jeans rubbing against my leg
So big and so very cool
Oh yes but
I got no bucks no lucks no pocket money blues

I could see myself fashion king with that top
So wicked, smart and snazzy the long-sleeved top
Oh yes but
I got no bucks no lucks no pocket money blues

I could see myself feeling the warmth of that hat
So slick and fresh
Oh yes but
I got no bucks no lucks no pocket money blues.

Ali Saad (11)
Pontarddulais Comprehensive School

First Day At School

First day at school,
What can I expect.
Dad calls me early,
Mum's a bit upset.

On the school bus,
First years at the front.
'You're not coming at the back'
The fifth formers have a grunt.

Who will be in my class?
A friend or two I hope.

Into the main hall,
Waiting to hear my name,
Emma is in another form,
That really is a shame.

Great I'm with Luke,
We're in Form 7T.
Room 3 is my form room
For registration that's where I'll be.

We're given lots of information,
Such a lot to learn.
Soon the day is over
The first day of the term.

Mum's waiting at the front door,
'How was it today James?'
'Great Mum, and the best thing
Is tomorrow we have games!'

James Frazer (11)
Pontarddulais Comprehensive School

THE MERMAID

I walk along the beach,
I see ripples in the water,
A tail quickly jumped over the clear blue sea,
She sat on a rock with her green seaweed hair,
Calling me, calling me, calling me.

I walked along the beach,
To the person or thing,
She kept calling me, calling me, calling me,
She grabbed me pulled me down under the water,
I sat on a dolphin it pulled me down, down, down.

The dolphin took me for a ride,
Down to the land of fish of colours.
The colours green, blue, yellow, red.
Rainbow of colour,
of stripes and zig zags.

Octopus, eels, jellyfish and whales,
Seemed to dance and sway,
Corals and shells of wonder,
Colours and shapes,
Made a carpet over the sea bed.

But suddenly I wake up,
It was all a dream,
The fish, the corals, the shells,
Were all pretend but the mermaid's voice,
echoed come with me, come with me, come with me.

Amy Davies (11)
Pontarddulais Comprehensive School

THE STORMY NIGHT

A loud crackle through the witch
A long loud howl the wolf cried
Then a little sigh of purring in the
Witch's den as a cat as black as night
Catwalked over to his black depressing crib.
Bubbling through a great big storm
Stirring round a spoon in a cauldron
The witch's magic spells and potions.
Then came a crash as loud as thunder
A large boot bigger than the Empire State Building
As the witch's cackle strikes again
As she looks up to see a hundred foot giant
Rising through the clouds.
On the broom she would go and fly
To a mad scientist's new invention - a body.
But who was it?
A flash of thunder struck the body.
It rose so that the cream coloured sheet
Fell off his face.
But who was it?
A scary-looking beast stared at them in fright,
A green face with bolts
Yes you've got it - Frankenstein.

Natalie Adams (11)
Pontarddulais Comprehensive School

ONE HOPEFUL WISH

There she was,
an angel in our midst,
but she only gave one hopeful wish.

I wish the world would be in peace,
And not one battle to the end of all life.

Before I could ask,
She was gone out of sight,
Without a whisper,
But one flash of light.

I hope she will come back,
I hope she will grant my wish,
Then I will give her one tiny kiss.

She did come back,
One day later,
With a halo on her head,
She was lying in bed.

She had died again,
From stress and weakness,
Now I know,
Just like me she was sweetness.

Bethan Turner (11)
Pontarddulais Comprehensive School

I Love Weekends

Weekends are just great
They are full of exciting hours ahead
I get lots of nice things to eat
And I have lots of my favourite treats

I like lots of things at the weekend
For instance I have my lye in
Thinking of my day ahead

My weekend is packed with exciting things
Like rugby, football, cricket and
Perhaps a swim

At the end of my great two days
I curl up and think of the next weekend.
Oh weekends are just great!

Aaron Shingler (11)
Pontarddulais Comprehensive School

The Black Cat

She stretches
Her small padded paws suddenly dangerous
Her claws spring out her small pink mouth yawns
With dagger sharp teeth like miniature stalactites in the cavernous deep
Her glossy coat shining black in the light
As she walks, shoulder blades moving, her sleek fur stretching
Seeming almost to glide, as her body twists and turns
Her green eyes with deep black pupils
Like whirlpools hold, hold me in a *spell!*

Annie Lee (11)
Pontarddulais Comprehensive School

SHOPPING

I love shopping,
It's really cool,
It's better than being
In the swimming pool.

Shopping with my friends,
It will never end,
But nothing is better,
Than shopping with my mother.

Shopping with my mother,
Is definitely the best,
Nothing can beat shopping,
With my mother.

Jordana Thomas (11)
Pontarddulais Comprehensive School

I LOVE THE SEA

I love the sea
Rough, strong, dark water
Smashing, crashing, tumbling waves
Deafening noise
Crashing against cliffs
Rushing away
Yes I love the sea.

I love the sea
Light, falling, blue water
Rolling, smoothing fall
Falling down on the sand
Yes I love the sea.

Emma Roberts (11)
Pontarddulais Comprehensive School

SPORTS

My main interests are bikes
I don't like going on hikes
whether they are long or short
they're not worth a thought
my favourite sport is bikes.

For fishing you have got to have bait
take your brother or even a mate
it's better than dancing
all that twirling and prancing
dancing is what I really hate.

I'll tell you what I really like, pool
I dream of playing in school
it's better than chess
I like chess less
and I'm good at playing the fool!

Finally, to finish swimming
which is usually done by women
my name is Tom
when I jump and bomb
my body all over starts stinging.

Tom Williams (11)
Pontarddulais Comprehensive School

STORM FAMILY

The icy grip of the rain,
Like millions of tentacles
Reaching for me.

The fiery wind like a crisp cold hand
Curling round everything
Reaching for me.

The stern thunder,
With its monstrous breath,
Shaking the Earth,
Reaching for me.

The lightning cracks,
Like a whip on the ice,
With its bright shock sensation,
Reaching for me.

And here I am,
All warm, snug and cosy,
With a family of storm
Waiting, waiting,
Reaching for me.

Robyn Lee Shefford (12)
Pontarddulais Comprehensive School

PONTARDDULAIS

Here is Pontaddulais, a village that's the tops,
it even has a Co-op and some corner shops.
If you want chips that are really nice,
take a tip from my friend, go to Paradise.
Salty, greasy, full of fat,
somehow I think you'll really like that.

There's the doctors, opticians and dentists too,
where they look after me and you.
Fancy a Mega Drive or PlayStation?
Pop down to Megabyte without hesitation.
Then there's Arwel's, Rhiannon's and Salon 2,
where you can get a style just for you.

On Saturday afternoon, I watch Bont play,
but when they lose I sneak away.
The Fountain, King and Farmers are here,
where you can buy a pint of beer.
But if you drink too much in the club,
the next stop for you is Tree and Gubb.

The Comp, the Primary and Bryniago,
are where Bont's children have to go.
English, maths and geography,
are just three things taught to me.
It's the first year in Comp for me,
I miss J4 where I used to be.

Adrian Hire (11)
Pontarddulais Comprehensive School

YOUNG LOVE

Their eyes meet across the classroom
Her heart pounds rapidly
Only one thing stands in their way
His life-long girlfriend.

She goes home every night
And cries herself to sleep
He sleeps with her
In a frame under her pillow.

She dreams of him
Of what he did
And of what he'd say
Indeed, she was hooked.

They become best friends
She smiles, no more tears
Yes, she is happy
He makes her happy.

As they get closer
Their friendship strengthens
Phone calls turn into secret riddles
Which only they know the answers.

She is scared, inexperienced
They grow fonder and fonder
Nothing will stop them now
They're in love.

Emily Chatfield (14)
Pontarddulais Comprehensive School

SCHOOL SCHEDULE

Maths is good,
English is not bad,
and playtime is to make the teachers mad.

Cooking is made to make a mess,
D and T is where we make a dress,
Art is where Van Gogh comes in handy,
So IT can't be handy.

PE is for football a glorious goal,
History is where we solve mysteries,
but Geography must be the subject not for me.

'Bonjour la classe', says Mr Arnold,
'Bore da', says Mrs Richards,
'Hello class', says Miss Salter,
which language shall I speak?

'Watch that Bunsen burner!' says Mr Bulger,
'Don't break that microscope!' says Mr C Jones,
Don't do this don't do that,
all these commands what shall I do?

So if you like work come to Bont comp,
But if you don't stay away from Bont comp.

Dylan Lewis (11)
Pontarddulais Comprehensive School

FIRST AND LAST

On the first day I was sad,
I was leaving Mum and Dad,
As I looked out the windowpane,
I thought I'd never see my mum again,
I watched my mum rub her hands with glee,
As she was free till half past three.

Mrs Bachelor short and sweet,
Mrs Ackroid never to meet,
Mrs Richards never-ending,
Gerald's job involves mending,
Mr Hedges I never had the pleasure,
Mr Harris always good for leisure,
Mrs Mathewson she is fine,
Mrs Roberts cheers me through the line,
Gail has a lollipop we can't lick,
Mrs Jones once gave me a tick,
Put together they're insane,
Don't know if I could do it again.

On the last day I am sad,
To be leaving - as I have had,
A great time in this school,
Thank you all
For my school life has been really cool.

Sam Richards (11)
Pontarddulais Comprehensive School

WHEN I GO FOR A WALK

The smell of the trees, the feel of the breeze
When I go for a walk,
The chance to chat and be relaxed
When I go for a walk,
The autumn breeze the fallen leaves
When I go for a walk,
The thick, black clouds and leaves in mounds
When I go for a walk,
The acorns forming upon the trees and now
The colder, harsher breeze
When I go for a walk,
No more squirrels scurrying along because
Now they're hibernating for very long
When I go for a walk,
The winter months dark and cold
And all the trees are looking old
When I go for a walk.

Sarah Richards (12)
Pontarddulais Comprehensive School

FRIENDS

Friends
Who are they?
What are they?
Are they people you can turn to?
People you can talk to?
People who you can care for?
Are they kind and caring
Or are the just fools?
Are they people who listen to your problems?
Do they have to be friendly to be your friend?

Friends are people who you love
Who you care for
Who you can talk to
They should be kind
They should be caring
Friends can be fools
They listen to your problems
A friend to me is all the above
What is a friend to you?
Friends.

Nicola Ann Lewis (13)
Pontarddulais Comprehensive School

TO MY PARENTS

To my parents the ones I love,
Who to me are a gift from above,
Thank you for being there when the going got tough,
And seeing me through with your love.
I know for a while we will still be apart
But you are loved deep within my heart,
The last few years I've put you through a lot
And you could have left me to rot,
But your love for me helped you through
And I promise you will never be blue.
Coz your love I can't bare to lose,
And I promise you again I will never abuse,
Your love to me that is so dear
Coz now I'm getting my head in gear
So goodnight and God bless Mum and Dad,
And I promise you again I will never be bad,
And now because I'm going, I'm going to be sad.

Kelly Richards (14)
Pontarddulais Comprehensive School

WATCHING

Whatever you do,
Whatever you say,
I'll still be there,
Day after day.

I'll be there,
There holding on,
My love for you,
Never gone.

I'll be your companion,
I'll be your friend,
I'll still be waiting,
Until the end.

Whenever you need me,
Need me to hold,
I'll still be loving,
When you are cold.

As I watch you,
On the hospital bed,
I'm still here,
My love unspoken, unsaid.

You won't know it,
But I am here,
Watching, waiting,
For a sign of life.

But now you are gone,
The tables have turned,
You watch me now,
From heaven.

I touch your gravestone worn and old,
Even though the sun is warm the marble
stays cold.

Eva Manning-Davies
Pontarddulais Comprehensive School

THE 'PERFECT' WORLD

The perfect world, full of perfect people,
All knowing exactly the same,
The perfect world, full of perfect people,
All looking exactly the same.

Each person, place and event,
Exactly like another,
Everyone looking perfect,
And the same as one another.

But could you live in a perfect world?
A land far from our reality,
Could you live the same as everyone else?
Having the same 'perfect' identity.

All perfectly formed and perfect in school,
With no differences and no ridicule.

No racism, no bullying, no hate and no fear,
It sounds a whole lot different,
From how we're living here.

Elisabeth James (14)
Pontarddulais Comprehensive School

I'M A CLOSED DOWN SCHOOL

I'm a closed down school on top of a hill.
I remember all the young children laughing
and having fun.
The old buzzer which used to go off
to tell the children to go to their next lesson.
The boys' football which used to hit my walls
and then bounce onto my roof.
The children's crisp packets that used to be pushed
into all the gaps and holes in my walls.
The headmaster's room that used to be filled
with naughty children.
The sound of his voice echoed through me as he shouted.
But now it's all quiet in his old room,
Another thing I miss is all the pins
that used to be pinned in my walls for
all the children's work.
I really miss being a part of the children's lives
and would love to be an open school again
and then I would be very happy.

Rhian Harris (11)
Pontarddulais Comprehensive School

THE BEACH

Strolling along the beach,
Sand brushing against my feet.
Waves splashing against the cliff,
The water bitter cold.

People swimming bravely in the water,
Lifeguards on the look out.
Boats sliding out from the harbour,
Fisherman trying to catch some fish.

Ice-cream vans selling ice-cream,
Driving along the beach.
Ambulances on the seaside,
For people who've been stung by jelly fish.

The people making sandcastles,
Looking at the rock pools.
The tide's coming in now,
And the people are starting to leave.

Samantha Lewis (13)
Pontarddulais Comprehensive School

MY CAT IS FAT

My cat is fat and all black
She eats and eats, that's all she does
She goes outside and chases birds
She goes inside and eats and eats
We stroke her and give her treats
My cat's name is Jessy
She is rather messy
She goes outside every day
She goes outside and plays in the hay
She chases mice and dogs all day
We call her in, she doesn't come
But soon remembers her tum
My cat does nothing right or wrong
She's thirteen years old
And sleeps all day long.

I love my cat
Even though she may be fat.

Lewis Baker (13)
Pontarddulais Comprehensive School

TENNIS

The players walk on the centre court
The crowd begin to cheer
The players finish their knock up
The beginning is coming near

The first ball is struck
And in the court it goes
The challenger is nervous
And the defending champion knows

Halfway through the match
The challenger takes the lead
The champion gets worried
And feels a burning need

The champion makes a comeback
And does it with style
The champion wins again
And bursts into a smile

What a great match
With action all the way
Everyone had a great time
On this momentous day

The championships are over
But celebrations still go on
All the players have left now
And all the crowds are gone.

Adam Rogers (13)
Pontarddulais Comprehensive School

EXTINCT!

Help!
Call out the animals,
Lizards and toads fleeing,
From the moist grounds.

Pandas with gloomy eyes,
Cling to trees for life,
Monkeys and gorillas,
Leap from tree to bush.

Nowhere to go,
Nowhere to hide,
People come to burn the forest,
Animals trapped.

The forests burn,
Animals sadly cry out,
Stop the burning,
Stop the fires.

The trees are dying,
Turning to ash,
The animals are suffering,
Slow and painful death.

Extinction, extinction . . .
                Extinct!

Emma Buckley (13)
Pontarddulais Comprehensive School

DIFFERENT

Anorexia,
It's so unthought of, you turn to a skeleton,
It kills, it hurts, I've no one to tell,
It makes my life a living hell,
Do you know how it feels to eat,
And then hide it under my bed-cover sheets?
But, if you look at my gaunt skin,
You'll find a person in me within.

I am black, he is white,
I am wrong, he is right,
I live in dark, he lives in light,
I am black, he is white,
They have fun and laugh at me,
I'm a slave, he is free.

I'm in the dark all alone,
No place I can call home,
I used to be home, unaware of the dangers,
Now I ask for money off strangers.

These are difficulties people must face,
No fault of their own, in the human race,
People must not condemn them,
That would make the world a better place.

Rob Nagi (13)
Pontarddulais Comprehensive School

THE MATCH

Excitement, passion, the thrill,
That's what fills the stadium,
Nervous, jumpy, pressure,
That's what the players feel.

Hope, loyalty, pleasure,
That's what the fans experience,
Zero tolerance, no messing about,
That's what the ref persists.

Stress, anxiety, tension, trauma,
That's what the managers go through,
The managers bring:
Relief, happiness, delight.

The ref brings:
Respect, pride,
The fans bring:
poverty, rejection, grimness.

The players bring:
Ease, aching,
The stadium brings:
Joy, glory, magnificence.

Keith Phillips (13)
Pontarddulais Comprehensive School

THE DREAM

What a game it was
It was the 90th minute
We were drawing one each against our arch rivals
We had to win to qualify
We were on the attack
And one of their players fouled one of our players
The referee said 'Free kick'
It was right outside the box
We had a good chance of scoring
So we went for it
He just belted it straight into the top corner
Gooooooaaaaal!
The crowd went mad
The players went mad
Even I went mad
Everybody went mad
The referee blew the final whistle
Everybody went mad again
But then something happened
Somebody started shouting 'Get up'
And I opened my eyes
And realised that it was just a dream
But it felt so real
Like it had happened
But it hadn't
'Oh well' I thought to myself
It was good while it lasted.

Jonathan Harris (13)
Pontarddulais Comprehensive School

WHY, MY MUM, WHY?

The dark was suffocating,
I couldn't sleep,
I strained my ears to hear more,
Even though I didn't want to.
A muffled whimper came from the next room
I was shaken and shivering,
It was my mum.
My mum was crying
But it was not normal
It sounded painful
My heart leapt as I heard her go to the bathroom.
Something was wrong
I had never heard her cry before
The noise of a tap screamed through the night sounds
When she settled back to bed I tried to sleep too
Impossible
My heart thumped!
Why was I so scared?
I tried to blank it from my mind,
And somehow I managed to sleep that night.
The next day I found out.
She sat me down,
And looked me in the eye,
She was ill.
The doctor said
She had to go to hospital,
It was infuriating.
Why, my mum? Why?
Why cancer? Why?

Siân Gray (13)
Pontarddulais Comprehensive School

HELEN

Helen lived in a small house.
At the tender age of two,
Her world turned as quiet as a mouse.
The world became dark and silent.
She was deaf and blind,
And often violent.
She could touch and smell,
And with her fingertips,
Feel the movement of her mother's lips.
No communication,
Led to frustration.
Then her teacher came,
And wrote words on her palm.
Slowly, she began to understand,
And Helen became calm.
Chains that had bound her were now broken.
From her mouth, sweet word were spoken.
She began to enquire and was curious,
But she was cautious and dubious.
Helen went to Norway for a week,
And heard of a girl with similar problems,
But had learnt to speak.
Helen was determined,
But it was a difficult task,
For she realised, she had a lot to ask.
The more she asked, the more she learned,
Until no longer she felt spurned.
For her perseverance she was happily rewarded,
And all her efforts were widely applauded.

Siân Cliff (13)
Pontarddulais Comprehensive School

HOLIDAY HOME

We had arrived.
We stepped out of the car,
It was sweltering the absolute opposite to a freezer,
I walked towards the clear clean pool,
It was ice-cold,
Everything was so beautiful, the aroma was lovely,
Lots of flowers in one.

Then I glanced at the garden that surrounded the house.

The house had dark brown tiles with creamy white bricks.
The shutters were a light brown which matched with the tiles well.

I strolled around the back while everyone else unpacked.

There was a tall wooden swing,
Which was surrounded by tiny plants.

'Michelle?'

I ran indoors to look round and to choose my room,
My bedroom was bright and colourful,
The living room was ugly compared to the outside,
It was as if I had been taken into a different world.

The kitchen was the best,
There was loads of food in the fridge,
There was a lovely long pine table with matching stools.

'Michelle???'

I switched off the video camera and answered to my mother.
'Coming.'

So much for exploring, I thought.

Michelle Huggleston (13)
Pontarddulais Comprehensive School

OH, WHAT ARE THEY FOR?

Little brothers,
What are they for?
Making a mess?
Throwing toys on the floor?

Winding me up,
All day and all night,
With snakes, frogs and spiders,
To give me a fright.

Laughing and joking -
Thinking they're funny,
To me, they're dirt-covered imps,
Their noses all runny.

Oh, they're a pain -
They drive me insane!
Causing mischief wherever they go,
Messing my room,
And squirting their guns,
'Til I'm soaked from head to toe.

Causing trouble,
And getting out of it, too!
Putting the blame on me,
They even set our hamsters loose,
Saying 'The hamsters want to be free!'

Little brothers,
Imps in disguise!
You'd never guess what they think of,
Under those innocent, blue eyes.

Kylie Hearne (12)
Pontarddulais Comprehensive School

SPANISH ISLES

On our holiday we went to Spain.
We didn't expect to get much rain.
When the plane landed and they opened the door,
What do you think greeted us? Yes, a down pour.
We collected our luggage and hopped on the bus,
The holiday rep was making a fuss.
The hour long journey to our hotel,
Saw windmills, palm trees, McDonald's as well.
On our arrival we checked into our room,
To be honest it wasn't a moment too soon.
Plenty of food to eat all day,
And the best thing was we didn't have to pay.
Tennis, crazy golf, horse riding too,
You could never say there was nothing to do.
On the lake you could go for a row,
If that didn't suit, take a pedalo.
Trips you could take if you fancied a change,
The one we liked most was the mountain range.
Evening time was always such fun,
My mum played bingo but never won.
At 9.30 on the dot,
The outdoor cinema was the best spot.
At the end of the film and on the way back,
We would always stop and have a snack.
The hardest part when the time drew near,
To say goodbye to my friends, we all shed a tear.
When we landed in Cardiff and got off the plane,
What do you think greeted us? Yes, more rain.
I enjoyed my holiday it was so cool,
The only thing now, it's back to school.

Louise Williams (13)
Pontarddulais Comprehensive School

WAITING

Opening the window to smell,
the fresh-aired morning.
Looking at the dew,
on the freshly cut grass.
Hearing all the people pass,
but muttering under their breath.
'Look at the house, it is such a mess.'
Knowing all the people know what you don't want them to know.
A bird sat on the windowsill
singing merrily along with a bluebird.
I called him in,
but he wouldn't come.
It all turned dark,
the sun had gone.
But I was still waiting,
waiting for him to come.

Katrina Grant (13)
Pontarddulais Comprehensive School

ALL ABOUT ME

My school uniform is all red, black and white,
My shoes are suede, rubber and black,
My pens and pencils for maths and other subjects,
My books are yellow, they were red in the past,
For drink I have a lot of pop,
When I get home I change straight out of my uniform,
I go to call for my friends,
We have a big game of football,
At half-time we all have a rest and talk to each other,
At full-time other people's mums call their children in for tea,
Then I end up going home for tea and after tea I go to bed.

My hair is fair,
My eyes are brown,
I'm 4ft 4 when you look down,
I have a dog, her name is Saffie,
She's a ball of white fluff and very crafty,
She brings her bowl when she wants food,
And puts my mum in a very bad mood,
At night when I pretend to sleep,
I open my eyes and take a peek,
And there is Saffie fast asleep!

Ashley Lewis (11)
Pontarddulais Comprehensive School

WHAT IS LOVE?

What is love?
Is it not a bird,
Eagle, lark or robin?
Nay.
It is the music beneath the moon,
And the song between the stars.
It is the sparkle in your eyes,
When the sun sets beneath the velvet sky.
And when the angels come to free
Your spirit into the dancing oceans,
When roses blossom into magic fairies,
Which give hope to every girl and boy.
It is the trees and animals,
Which praise the light of the smiling world.
And the hills and mountains,
Which send memories of joy and happiness.
Love is the mystery beyond,
The crystallised sea of beauty.

Sharon Louise Jones (14)
Pontarddulais Comprehensive School

MY DOG!

My dog Trixie,
She is very small,
She walks all day,
And sleeps all night,
And eats on her breaks.

She's black and white,
With some brown,
And acts all nice and soppy.

She likes her food,
And beef stew,
With some lamb and chicken.

My father chucks her out,
We bring her in,
He gets angry,
We all scream.

She's long and lean,
Sweet and playful.

We all love her,
And she loves us.

Ruth Taylor (13)
Pontarddulais Comprehensive School

LONELINESS

A breeze of cold,
Of the story I told,
A winter morning,
As the sun was dawning.

The wind blowing over the meadow,
Someone's voice calling me like a bellow,
I'm lonely as that voice has gone,
Now I'm all alone.

Wandering day by day,
Which way do I go, which way, which way?
The mist is calm and gentle,
Like the sea whispering a melody.

A gentle silence lay over the beach,
A gentle wave as the sea laps onto the shore,
As it was saying hello,
A calm whisper from side to side.

A coldness climbing up my spine,
And here I say another time,
I'm lonely as can be,
Like the coldness of the sea.

Joanne Leddy (13)
Pontarddulais Comprehensive School

THE CHAMPIONS

I like playing basketball
It is pretty fun
I like shooting hoops
My favourite player is 'Jordan'
He averages 40 points
And jams every game
He plays for Chicago
Chicago Bulls that is
With team mates 'Scottie' and 'Denis'
They are simply unstoppable!
Their coach is Phil Jackson
And he is six foot tall
They win every game by
10 points or more
Sometimes they score at the very end
Then 'Jordan' takes over the game
And scores at the buzzer
Sometimes fakes right sometimes left
Then he pulls up the shot
Buzz!
The 'Bulls' win!

Jason Elvins (13)
Pontarddulais Comprehensive School

GHOST

Up on the deserted mountain
lies something,
something quiet,
something white,
something that will give you a fright!
It is a ghost,
not a friendly one,
but a spooky, lurking, ghostly ghoul!

One dark night a lost traveller,
had a frightening experience,
he wished that just once,
he could be home, eating cream on scones,
because the ghost *appeared* from nowhere!
The lone traveller tried everything,
screaming and shouting from a great height,
but the ghost just lead him into the night.

Nicola Davidson (11)
Pontarddulais Comprehensive School

A TASTE OF AUTUMN

There is a taste of autumn in the air,
when,
the leaves trickle to the ground like
a stream running
down a hill.
When,
the sun in the sky shines down like a
golden coin.
When,
the wind twirls round and round
like a whirlwind with a
sound.
When,
the animals start collecting food for
their winter store.
When,
the silver star shines bright
helping people to see in the night.
Freshly made and full of flavour,
autumn's a time I like to savour.

Daniel Hennah (12)
Pontarddulais Comprehensive School

FOOTBALL IS THE BEST

F ree kick has just been taken
O h
O h the crowd shout as
T he
B all hits the post
A ll the attackers
L unge for the ball
L uis Enriqué kicks the ball away

I t falls at
S chmeichels feet he picks it up

T he big Dane kicks it up-field
H enningberg heads it on
E ventually it gets to Beckham

B eckham takes on Rivaldo and produces an
E xtraordinary cross to Paul Scholes
S choles puts a brilliant ball through to the
T rinidad and Tobago International Dwight Yorke who scores and wins the game.

Chris Watkins (13)
Pontarddulais Comprehensive School

ME!

My hair is long and fuzzy,
My eye's are black and thin.
My shoes are out of fashion
So I chucked them in the bin.

My feet are double jointed,
My legs are thin and sleek.
I wish I had a brain left
'Cos I've got two left feet.

My chest is wide and hairy,
My bellybutton's deep.
My lips are small and bubbly
So it's hard to get some sleep.

My toes are small and lumpy,
My teeth are goofy and green.
My ears are full of ear wax
And there's nothing of mine that's clean.

Carl Mainwaring (13)
Pontarddulais Comprehensive School

OLD TRAFFORD

Old Trafford is the greatest ground's name,
Holding fifty-six thousand seats.
It is a landmark in Greater Manchester
And home to the great team.

Legends used to play there like
Only the best!
One of them was George who could out run the rest,
But now we see players emerging,
Like Beckham, Giggs and Cole,
And hear the crowd roar, as they score a goal.

Inside the football palace the atmosphere is amazing,
Seeing all the seats,
So many red, red seats.

When you see a football game,
It is the greatest sight,
Because even when it's pouring,
United still keep scoring!

Stephen Liddiard (12)
Pontarddulais Comprehensive School

CATS

Cats sleep
Anywhere,
Any table,
Top of piano,
Window ledge,
In the middle,
On the edge,
Open drawer,
Empty shoe,
Anybody's
Lap will do,
Fitted in a
Cardboard box,
In a cupboard
With your frocks
Anywhere!
They don't care!
Cats sleep
Anywhere.

Rhian Williams (11)
Pontarddulais Comprehensive School

MY MUM

My mum's short, plump and pretty and I wish
she'd give up slimming.
Her cooking is delicious but you can hardly eat it,
The way she looks at you eating her cooking,
When all she has is a tasteless biscuit.

My dad thinks so too,
She cooks and cleans and irons and plays the part
of mum but,
She lives on tasteless biscuits,
And she is the best mum in the world but,
my mum's short and plump and pretty and I wish
she'd give up slimming.

Rachael Stephens (12)
Pontarddulais Comprehensive School

THE BEACH

Sunny sandy
Deep blue sea
Fish grabs seaweed
The sun shining down
On the golden sand
Footprints on the marked
Hurt sand
In the winter sand moves
Forced to a new spot
Poor sand
People running wild
Washed away forever
The sea crashing against the rocks
Like a hurricane
The sand in people's eyes
Blind forever
No one knows the beach
Like I do
The pieces of wood
Like a sea monster
I love the beach.

Penny Davies (12)
Pontarddulais Comprehensive School

COOL CARS

It's got alloy wheels
It's got a huge exhaust
Its speed is amazing
It's long round shape
Such a quiet engine
It's a
Ford RS Cosworth

Lovely red colour
Really fast speed
Golden alloy wheels
Its really big engine
It looks really cool
It's a
Ferrari Testarossa

It's a rally car
Wild blue and yellow colour
Gold wheel spokes
Brilliant tyre grip
Brilliant handling
It's a
Subaru Impreza.

Simon Pearce (12)
Pontarddulais Comprehensive School

AT NIGHT

At night
When I go to bed at night I hear
All these strange sounds
I get out of bed to see what it is
As I open the curtains there
Is nothing there to see.

Thinking in bed to myself of
All the things I could think of
Then suddenly snap it came to me.
It's most probably the wind blowing
Through the trees and all the leaves
Falling down swiftly.

Catherine Gwenter (12)
Pontarddulais Comprehensive School

MY CHRISTMAS LIST

Dear Santa
For Christmas I want a boat
No I don't, I want a horse
Or a bike
Help me Santa, I don't know what I'd like.

I want a go-kart like everyone else
That is it!
A computer game
But which one?
There are so many.

Clothes! That's an idea
Adidas, Nike or Reebok
What about rollerskates
Or maybe some CDs.

Or maybe . . . Na, I know what they'd say
Santa isn't a millionaire
Yes but he is a magician
Maybe he'll get me something I'd like
Football boots
Size 8 please Santa.

Liam Coleman (13)
Pontarddulais Comprehensive School

The Castle

Looming over the town,
In the dead of night,
The witching hour,
The cold stone floor,
Rough turned smooth,
Worn by many shoes,
Trooping up the long, narrow stairs,
The walls seem to creak and groan,
Crying out,
As if they have an aching limb,
Sore from people leaning against the stone,
To rest their feet,
Listen carefully,
Ssh . . .
The walls seem to whisper,
Whisper secrets,
Legends never to be told,
Tourists move uncaringly through the castle,
Feeling the bleak cobbled walls,
Seeing the dirty, overgrown gardens,
Smelling the musty, damp air,
They now see the castle as a mere tourist attraction,
When if you look closely you'll see it has magic,
It has beauty,
An amalgamation of perplexity and pain.

Wendi James (13)
Pontarddulais Comprehensive School

FOOTBALL FEVER

Football is my favourite game,
I play in the sun and in the rain,
My favourite team is Liverpool,
They make the others look like fools.

I support them through think and thin,
Even though they don't always win,
But when they do I go to school with a grin.

I'd play football anytime, anywhere,
In a park, in a street, I don't care,
My team is Kingsbridge Colts, they're simply the best,
The mighty, mighty troop's better than the rest.

Every weekend, to Kingsbridge Park I go,
And take my place between the posts,
I hope the team aren't feeling low.

Oh! Come on ref, give the whistle a blow,
Or they'll soon score another goal,
You can't let him go for that,
It's in the rule book and that's a fact.

But it's too late now,
Our time is up,
Dave is going to give us a blow,
And maybe decide,
The defence has to go,
So wake up midfield, score some goals.

Mark Corcoran (13)
Pontarddulais Comprehensive School

THE BEACH

Waves crashing against the rocks
Wind ripples across the sand
Sun shining over the sea
The feeling is great
The ice-cream melting down the cone
All over you before you get a chance
Mums shouting at little girls
Dads sleeping and can't be bothered
Children having fun building sandcastles
Other children knocking them down
Nannas dipping toes in the water
They jump back because it's too cold
People drifting out
People burnt screaming and shouting
Mums going for a swim
Tell children don't go too far
One little boy going in the water
Shivering as he walks towards it
He's running back - can't go in -
Back and forth, back and forth
Look, he's in the sea!

Samantha Rees (12)
Pontarddulais Comprehensive School

THE BLIND MAN

A blind man can't see,
Who is asleep and starts a dream,
He has to walk with a stick,
People ask him, 'Can you see any light?'
'Well yes, of course, I see
the light of the stars above
my head,' said the blind man
Just sitting there.

'I wish that a person
Like you could help me see again.
I have a dream,
To live like a normal person,
I wish someone
Could help me see the world again.'
The worst to come
Has gone away
But now my dream
Has ended
I have to wait and see.

Tabitha Ford (13)
Pontarddulais Comprehensive School

THE BEES BEATS

The wind is blowing through the trees,
I can hear it, it sounds like bees.
The leaves think they are the *bee's knees*
They listen to the Bee Gees.
The bees dance to the Bee Gees' beats.
They jump around and stamp their feet.

If bees had hands instead of wings,
I wonder if that would, change things.
They would clap around dance and sing.
And do all sorts of new things.
With these new hands that they've just found,
There's just no telling what is around.

Some bees can spin and some can jive,
They buzz about till they find the hive.
They look for pollen when the days are sunny
For feeding babies and their mummy.

Sarah Brown (12)
Pontarddulais Comprehensive School

HERE I AM WITHOUT A HOME

Here I am without a home
No one love me -
I'm all alone.

Here I am without a home
I'm so hungry
Eating off bones.

Here I am without a home
I'm so cold
In these old clothes.

Here I am without a home
In a cold box
My only home.

Here I am without a home
I don't belong
Where will I go
Please help me!

Leyah Hillman (13)
Pontarddulais Comprehensive School

AUTUMN

Don't sound the flute!
Make everything mute.
All the leaves are dead,
And all the animals are abed.
Merrily, merrily the year is starting to end.

When children are playing in the fallen leaves,
And through the trees the wind weaves,
The sky above and grass below,
And autumn winds now do blow.
Merrily, merrily the year is starting to end.

Golden-brown crops like autumn's hair,
In autumn the skies are fair.
The sun is like a big red ball,
And now the autumn leaves do fall.
Merrily, merrily the year is starting to end.

Yellow, orange, crimson and brown,
Now winter is here people do frown.
The air is very so bitter,
And the snow covers the litter.
Sob, sob autumn has ended.

Matthew Brooks (11)
Pontarddulais Comprehensive School

THE REALLY SCARED GHOST!

'The poor thing' Miss Goulish cried.
He thinks his eggs are terrifried!
He's really scared of everything.
His nose, his eyes, even his ring.
He really is a wimp you know.
Even though he's got a heart.
I really know what I should do
After tea he's having a lesson or two!
Then he'll have to practise practise
practise he knows that it makes perfect
Then later on he was not so scared
Now he was really scary!
Now we just can't stop him he's much
too scary
Now he needs to pack it in
He's doing our heads right in!

Michael Cooper (12)
Pontarddulais Comprehensive School

SKIING

Skiing,
It's an amazing thing,
Only 4 in 10 are likely to try it,
To be good at skiing takes a lot,
At first it takes a tremendous amount of effort,
But after a while,
Of falling on your . . . behind,
You can step up a stage and,
Take it as an exhilarating ride,
But don't get too confident because,
You might end up falling on your . . . behind.

I like to glide,
Swiftly down a fresh pack of snow,
I love skiing, I'll have you know,
I go skiing every year,
I look forward to it more then,
When Santa's knocking on my door,
I go skiing in Pemprey,
Nearly every Saturday,
But I'd much rather be going as fast as I can,
Down a steep, fresh patch of snow,
I'll have you know.

Daniel Jones (12)
Pontarddulais Comprehensive School

CADILLAC

I stand in a factory all deserted and gone
Crumbling away and falling down
But once this was a thriving place.
This was the Cadillac manufacturing place.

The best car ever made
Designed to a tee
So beautiful and sleek
And over seven feet long
The best to the greatest degree.

I once had a Caddy
Blue like a hawk
It purred so nice
The greatest ever made.

Now it's gone, taken for scrap
How sad I was!
Then I saw it crashed, crushed away
Never to return again
I will never forget the most
Outstanding car in the world.
My Cadillac
Gone forever.

Robert Courtney (12)
Pontarddulais Comprehensive School

GLORIOUS FOOD

I like to eat
My favourite, is pizza and ham.
I'm not really fussy on lamb.
I also like brown bread called bran.
I even like a bit of Spam.
But nothing beats a bit of ham.

I like all food, sweets and cakes.
And sometimes my mother likes to bake,
But sometimes it gives me a tummy ache.

So we go shopping once a week,
To get all my favourites I like to eat.
I like fruit, apples, grapes, peaches,
Only thing I don't like is tin peaches.

Vegetables like sprouts, swede and peas,
But eating the vegetables I'm not very pleased.
But at the end of the day,
I just love food.

Adrian Paton (11)
Pontarddulais Comprehensive School

THE WATERFALL

The waterfall sparkling in the sun,
Hitting the rocks with a giant thump,
As strong as a bear.
But at the bottom, calm and still,
Flowing through the stream with hardly a movement.

Above the stream the rough rivers flow,
Suddenly it goes down and down,
Bang as it hits the ground!
People are fishing too and looking in a cave
It is fun around the waterfall.

As high as a mountain, as steep as a cliff,
The waterfall looks beautiful,
Rocks and trees around the sparkling waterfall.
It starts to rain *tip-tap, tip-tap,*
As it hits the bottom.

Jason Lee Cole (11)
Pontarddulais Comprehensive School

SPOT THE DOG

There was a dog called Spot
He had a friend called Dot
They went for a walk
Found a good sport
Sat in the shade
Ate and ate
They went back home
They both ate a bone
Spot had a dose
When Dot had a repose
Spot woke up
Dot arouse
Started to bark
Spot barked back
Both were barking
Dot had a bone to calm down
Spot had food
The owner of Spot came out and said
'What's all this noise?'
Dot went back to doze
Spot went and had a snooze.

Kelly Mainwaring (13)
Pontarddulais Comprehensive School

A Rose In A Daffodil Field
(A Tribute To Princess Diana)

She was a good person,
Why did it happen to her?

You could see it coming,
Being followed everywhere she went.

She was a good person,
Why did it happen to her?

Our lives will never be the same without her,
Gone forever like a blown-out candle.

She was a good person to us,
You were a good person to everyone,
Why Diana? Why you?

Nicholas Morgan (12)
Pontarddulais Comprehensive School

Healthy Eating

I eat food all day long,
so I'll grow up to be healthy and strong.
Lots of fruit is good for me,
especially oranges with vitamin C.
Milk is good for teeth and gums,
I drink a glass when the milkman comes.
Plenty of vegetables and small green peas
don't have many calories.
Cod and plaice are tasty fish,
they make a very healthy dish.
So if you want to live a long life,
eat this food and save yourself strife.

Karen Lewis (13)
Pontarddulais Comprehensive School

BUMBLEBEE

Bizzy bee, bumblebee, buzzing all the time
Bizzing everywhere you go.

Bumbering and thumberling all the day long
Making honey to fill up your tummy and
to eat in straight lines.

Bizzing bee, buzzing bee, pollenating all around.

Two make plants grow around, and the
Bizzy bee will you please make me delicious
honey for me and my mother for tea and crumpets.

Bizzy bee, bumblebee, buzzing all over
the land to find your mummy and her honey
to make for you and my tummy.

Stephen Howells (14)
Pontarddulais Comprehensive School

FAIRIES

There's fairies at the bottom of our garden
Well that's what mum said
She said they all lived there in a tiny flower bed
Some fairies are happy
Some are sad
And some are cheeky
And really quite bad
Some fairies like the sun
Some like the rain
And some like to watch the hail on the windowpane
Now fairies are quite hard to find
And will only be seen by someone kind.

Charlotte Whalen (12)
Pontarddulais Comprehensive School

AT THE BEACH

The sand is warm and crispy
As the sand gets into your sandwiches
The water is sometimes cold
But other times it's warm
You're lovely and warm as you put on your lotion
You smell ice-cream
And hear seagulls
The waves crashing against the rocks
And the smell of seaweed
As you walk along the beach
The sun on your face
And the sun on your back
Ow!
And look at the litter
Look at the place
What a *mess!*

Sarah Treviso (12)
Pontarddulais Comprehensive School

AUTUMN

Golden leaves drop to the floor creating a carpet for the forest ground.
Squirrels dash around collecting nuts for the winter.
A chilly frost has gathered on the leaves and bare branches.
Flocks of birds are flying south as the bitter coldness sets in.
As night falls the foxes come out and howl into the midnight sky.
The bare branches create a silhouette against the pale winter moon.
The badgers doze in the undergrowth.
Everyone is getting ready for the winter and the cruel,
                                        bitter cold it brings with it.

Steven Card (12)
Pontarddulais Comprehensive School

Weather

Everything's snowed over
Even all the deep green leaves
Icicles lay around us
Jagged and zigzaggedly seen.

The sweltering summer has come
Which diffused all the ice
No more bleak and parky days
Time to see the mice.

There's also that fine cordial weather
With cold gusty breezes
But the deep orange leaves
Begin to discolour.

The autumn time has come
All the leaves lay on the ground
Dull, dark and dry
Not one green to be found.

The springtime is here
Jolly and exciting time of year
Cute bunnies jump around
Lower growing in the ground.

Catherine Stilwell (12)
Pontarddulais Comprehensive School

THE FAT BLACK CAT

My black cat
Was a very fat cat
And a very fat cat he was
He was such a greedy cat he ate all
The robins and the sparrows and the crows
Now my black cat
Had a very bright hat
That attracted all the birds from the sky
The cat gave the birds coffee, biscuits and tea
The fat cat pretended to be their friend
He fed them up, 'til they were very fat
But now the birds couldn't fly
Then he grabbed them with his claws
And gobbled them up
And now the fat cat
Is getting fatter and fatter every day.

Fay Mogford (13)
Pontarddulais Comprehensive School

MY PET STRESS

My pet Stress
is a pest.
He eats my food
and chews my shoes
and that's why he's a pest.

My pet Stress
does my tests
but shh no one knows
except for you
and that's why he's a pest.

My pet Stress
makes a mess
and leaves it on my desk
I got the blame
and that's why he's a pest.

My pet Stress
is neatly dressed
he wears a hat
can you imagine that?
and that's why he's a pest.

Vicki Erasmus (11)
Pontarddulais Comprehensive School

BEST THINGS

Coke from the fridge,
Bananas,
Cherries,
Mum when she's had a couple of sherries,
Ice-cream and jelly,
Nearly everything on telly,
Cartoons,
Westerns,
Comedy,
Pop,
Start on that I'll never stop,
The taste of parsley,
Vinegar,
Mustard,
School chocolate pudding,
With green custard.

James Rogers (13)
Pontarddulais Comprehensive School

BACKSTAGE

Peeping through the curtains,
Is there anybody there?
There's five hundred there for certain,
Now it's time to do our hair.

Upstairs in the dressing room,
Sitting by the mirror,
We're putting on our make-up,
Spraying our hair with glitter.

Costumes hanging on the rails,
Starting to get dressed now.
Cards arriving with the mail,
Flowers being delivered, *wow!*

Dancers check their laces,
Singers practice scales.
Producers put us through our paces,
Children start to wail.

We're all ready in the wing,
With costumes bright and bold.
As the chorus starts to sing,
The footlights shine a beam of gold.

__Angharad Evans (12)__
__Pontarddulais Comprehensive School__

SECRET ADMIRER

I'm thinking of you every day,
Even in my sleep,
I would even pay,
For you to say you're mine to keep.

Everywhere I go,
I'm thinking of you,
I wish I could tell you,
I wish that you knew.

To me you're like a burning flame,
You make my world go round,
I even adore your name,
You're the only love I've ever found.

You make my emotions run wild,
You're my everything,
Everyone says I'm just a child,
They say it's just a fling.

Ever since I saw your face,
I can't get you out of my mind,
My heart beats at such a pace,
You are just my kind.

Elaine Speyer (12)
Pontarddulais Comprehensive School

School Dinners

Rumbling tummies waiting in anticipation
as the wonderful aroma of freshly
baked pizza fills their nostrils
and tickles their taste buds.

Cheese bubbling like hot lava from a
volcano. The biting pepperoni inviting
and tempting the moaning and groaning
bellies in the ever-growing snake-like
dinner queue of ravenous children,
shuffling and pushing awaiting the
sound of the bell, like a gunshot in a race
Bbbbrrrrr!

The stampede begins!

Victoria Davies (12)
Pontarddulais Comprehensive School

The Three Billy Goats Gruff

When the goats are trotting by
the troll looks up and gives a cry,
get off my bridge you ugly things,
or you'll be on my plate for dins.

The smallest and the naughtiest of all went
trotting by with no fear at all,
the troll looked up and huffed and puffed
and shouted to the smallest billy goat gruff.

The billy goat gruff didn't like what he said
so he ran right home and went to bed.

Stephanie Dew (12)
Pontarddulais Comprehensive School

SKATES (JUMPS AND GRINDS)

Jumping through the air
grinding across curbs
safety grab in the air
do royal over there

Saying that is fair
wearing baggy clothes
for skate wear
wear good make for skating

Do one 180s
and do 360s
and try to go 540s
at least try.

Craig Cox (12)
Pontarddulais Comprehensive School

FLOWERS ARE A GIFT

Flowers are so beautiful,
They are a gift to see,
Their colours form a pattern bright,
A gift for you and me.
Such beauty is bewildering,
Shapes are varied too,
And often you will want to pick,
A bunch for me and you.
Such tiny plants that one will sow,
Begin just from a seed,
And gradually the seed will grow,
For all the world to see.

Adele Boobier (13)
Pontarddulais Comprehensive School

HOLIDAY

I want to go on holiday
I want to go real far
I want to go by aeroplane
Not by train, or car.

I want to go where it is hot
Where I can find a sunny spot
To laze around and sleep all day
To while the hour far away.

I want to see the fish in the sea
I want to laugh and swim with glee
Because I feel this way today
I need to go on holiday.

I want to go to Florida
And ride in a limousine car
And wave at people as I pass by
Then shout at them 'I've won the lottery.'

This is how I came today
To book the time so far away
Over in America
I'll travel on a cable car.

So I'm leaving this boring house
To go and see Mickey Mouse
Then in time I'll got to Rome
But eventually I'll come home.

Sean Owens (12)
Pontarddulais Comprehensive School

SEEING RED

The referee was a hated man,
he played the game without a fan.
He brought the red card out,
but I never gave that bloke a clout.

I lost my temper halfway through,
the grass was green, the air was blue.
The referee came charging down,
his face was stern and in a frown.

The player was lying very still,
he looked to me to be quite ill.
He had a nasty lump on his head,
and could have done with a week in bed.

The trainer came with a magic sponge,
and a pot of greeny, yellow gunge.
He was smiling because they'd nearly won,
apart from the ref we'd all had fun.

The boy got up and shook my hand,
at least I know where I stand.
'It was an accident,' he said,
It's not your fault I hurt my head.'

The referee would have none of this,
a booking he just could not miss.
He walked away a lonely man,
and I showered off with a three match ban!

Jack Matthews (12)
Pontarddulais Comprehensive School

THE FINAL

When we won the final,
The day I won't forget,
The whole team got stinking drunk,
And still aren't sober yet.

Our keeper Jimmy's brilliant,
He kept us in the match,
We thought that they were going to score,
But he did a great catch.

I'm really proud of this day,
It was a great game,
I thought I scored a decent goal,
And that's my claim to fame.

In the first ten minutes,
The ref didn't give a pen,
Then our striker missed the target,
And we all shouted *'Oh Ken!'*

The manager Bill,
He was really excited,
He made us the best,
And now we are delighted.

Nathan Evans (12)
Pontarddulais Comprehensive School

I Love You!

I hear the ticking of the clock
I wonder where you are tonight.
My love for you is still unknown
The secret lives in me.
You don't know how long I have wanted
to touch your lips and hold you tight.
I think about every night, I close my eyes
and there you are.
The very first time I saw your blond hair
and cute face, I knew you were perfect for me.
Whenever I see you I just wish
you would hold me in your arms and
whisper the words I love you.
I can't help these tears from falling
from my eyes when I know there's
no chance of you being mine.
I will never find another lover sweeter
and more precious than you.
You are the one that lives in me
and some day you shall know
how I really feel about you
how much I love you.

Sadie Thomas (13)
Pontarddulais Comprehensive School

A Pie In The Sky

I had a dream
That way up high
In the big blue sky
There was a big fat pie
A blackberry pie
Or was it an apple pie?
No it was a blackberry pie
I was afraid
The big fat pie
In the big blue sky
Was going to fall
In my big blue eye
And make me cry
Oh no it was a dream
No pie and cream
I want to scream
No blackberry pie
To fall in my eye
From way up high
In the big blue sky
I think I'll cry.

Nathan Raddenbury (11)
Pontarddulais Comprehensive School

The Haunted House

Cold and dark on a winter's day,
In a little street a haunted house lays.
Everything's quiet and still,
Watch out you might get killed.

Outside the house there are some graves,
Dead flowers and grass all over the paves.
We enter the house with a shake,
Ahhhh! Watch out for the rake.

Dust all over the floors,
Cobwebs all over the doors.
As we tread up the stairs,
Our hearts start trembling as we dare.

Onwards and upwards as we go,
Swinging backwards to and fro,
Nervous twitching, it's time to go.

Fallon Kift (13)
Pontarddulais Comprehensive School

BORN TO SHOP

I am a girl, born to shop,
Every day I cannot stop,
With my money I march to town,
All day long I don't sit down,
Every store in town I try,
Everything I see I buy,
Earrings, clothes, rings and hats,
Pens and books and dogs and cats,
The one thing I love above all,
When I see them I scream and call,
The one hobby I will never lose,
Is my dreadful love for shoes,
I leave the poor bank man crying,
To make me stop he is still trying,
But sorry, no, until that day,
There is nothing left to say,
Except . . .
Thanks to Marks and Sparks and Boots,
Miss Selfridge, Top Shop, what a hoot,
So this day on I vow not to drop,
'Cos I am a girl who is born to shop!'

Emma Black (11)
Pontarddulais Comprehensive School

MEAT MADNESS

I was walking down the street
When I found a piece of meat
I picked it up and said
'That's bigger than my head'
I took it home with me
I hung it from a tree
I took it in the house
And hid it from the mouse
I put it on the plate
And left it there till eight.

I had a round of golf
With my best friend Rolf
I was on the ninth hole
When I saw a huge mole
As I went to the bar
I saw someone stealing my car
I chased him down the street
With my poor aching feet
I reported it to the police
And then I told my niece

By the time I got back home
Someone had broken my garden gnome
I went into the house
And I looked for the mouse
Then I looked for the meat
But I found a piece of wheat
I rung my friend Ben
To meet him at our den
I was walking down the street
When I found a piece of meat.

Kayleigh Watkins (11)
Pontarddulais Comprehensive School

WHEN MRS COX HAD CHICKENPOX

Our school was pretty dull
The teachers never smiled at all
And the pupils never ran
You might say our class
Was the only normal one.

We had the best teacher of all
Her name was Mrs Cox
One day she didn't come to school
So we phoned her house
And found out she had chickenpox.

This little kid in our school
His sister had them
And when she came to school one day
Mrs Cox went far too near her
So she had them too.

We had to have a substitute
'Cause she couldn't come to school
Her name was Mrs Jones
The boys thought she was cool
And every day they stayed behind after school.

The next day she was really stressed
And began to rub her face
What we saw next we thought was funny
She must have had a mask on
Because now she looked so ugly.

She went up to the mirror
And her face turned red
As she ran out of the room
And funnily enough
We never saw her again.

Nerys Clement (11)
Pontarddulais Comprehensive School

I Wish I Had

Have you ever seen
A red and blue cow?
Have you ever seen
A green and yellow sheep?
Have you ever seen
A singing tomato?
Have you ever seen
A shark swimming in a river?
Have you ever seen
A monkey in a swamp?
Have you ever seen
A blue banana?
Have you ever seen
A banana sleeping?
Have you ever seen
A five legged lizard?
Have you ever seen
A 3 headed toad?
       I wish I had.

Matthew Sibley (11)
Pontarddulais Comprehensive School

Life!

I wish life was so easy
No homework that would be cool
We could sit around watching TV
Or we could sit or jump in the swimming pool

I wish life was easy
Doing whatever you want
You can hang around with friends
And go wherever you want

Or maybe life isn't so easy for people
They work to get money or go to school
Children walk miles and miles to go to school
Not like you or me

We walk not so far, or go in a car
Or maybe go on a bus, to us there is no fuss
I think I'll be grateful for what I've got
Compared to people who have not.

Nicola Hearne (12)
Pontarddulais Comprehensive School

MY GARDEN

My garden gives me pleasure with
Nice smells and flowers to see
My garden is my playground in my imagination
Whatever I want it to be
My garden a haven for God's creatures
Big and small
My garden is a sunbed for my cats
Who sunbathe on the wall
My garden is a wonder with soil and plants and trees
My garden is a piece of heaven for
Mam, dad and me
My dad he has a fish pond, it's his pride and joy
He loves to feed his fish
To see them swim and jump
My mam she loves the garden
She grows herbs to eat and smell and bathe in
Her flowers all year round are a great display
I love my garden to look at and play in or to have fun
My garden a haven for mam and dad and me.

Oliver Richards (11)
Pontarddulais Comprehensive School

PERFECT PASTIMES

In the evening when I'm free
I like to sit and watch TV.
Sunny days I also like
To play outside on my bike.
Me and dad have a lark
When we play tennis in the park.
My mum says 'It's books you need,'
Because she knows I like to read.
I like to go and play netball
But sometimes I trip up and fall.
I have a rabbit as a pet
And my dad, he likes to bet
That one day he'll run away
But I think he likes to stay.
He thinks his hutch is a very nice home
So he's not entitled to roam.
He likes to go into my little hut
So I keep the door firmly shut.
I must stop now so I can see
My favourite programmes on TV.

Angela Brugnoli (11)
Pontarddulais Comprehensive School

FOOD

Through the teeth
Past the gums
Looks out stomach
Here it comes.

I am hungry
As hungry as can be
I'm making a noise
Like a bumblebee.

I love food
Food loves me
We're a happy family.

Pardon me for being so rude
It was not me it was my food
It just popped up to say hello
Then it went back down below.

Jenna Edwards (12)
Pontarddulais Comprehensive School

THEY ARE NOT BETTER THAN US!

Red, yellow, brown and black
It's a chicken, can you see?
It goes cluck, cluck, cluck,
Cluck, cluck, cluck.
They're different from you and me.
We go chatter, chatter, chatter,
And they go cluck, cluck, cluck.
But can't you notice
They pluck themselves.
We don't!
We can swim
They must cling onto things
Travel on their wings.
We have queens and kings
What do they have? Nothing
Unlike them we don't lay eggs
Unlike us they don't have birthday parties
So my point is they may have wings
And other things
But that doesn't mean they're better than us.

Rebecca Collins (11)
Pontarddulais Comprehensive School

GYM

When gym begins in the morning,
When we are playing sport,
The teacher he is snoring,
Before the lesson is taught.

He takes the register, he never has a pen,
He likes to talk to all his friends,
He always whistles at half-time,
He tells the goalie to take his time.

I love football and cricket too,
Rugby's okay when you are wearing the shoes,
Badminton's great and basketball also,
I love sport and my friends too.

All the boys get dirty,
All the girls are clean,
They run to the shower,
And hope they're in the team.

We all get changed,
And go to the loo,
Have a drink,
And enjoy it too.

The teacher calls us out,
And makes us sit down,
Tells us to shut up,
We all put a frown on.

Kieran Downing (11)
Pontarddulais Comprehensive School

RAINFORESTS

Chop, chop, chop,
Down come the trees,
Chop, chop, chop,
Stop now please.

Cut, cut, cut,
Down come more,
Cut, cut, cut,
It should be against the law.

Burn, burn, burn,
Animals losing homes,
Burn, burn, burn,
There's nothing left but bones.

Dig, dig, dig,
Deep into the ground,
Dig, dig, dig,
There's nothing to be found.

Money, money, money,
That's what it's all about,
Money, money, money,
Shouldn't someone shout.

Sad, sad, sad,
There's not much left there now,
Sad, sad, sad,
The question must be - how?

Elinor Lewis (11)
Pontarddulais Comprehensive School

HAVE YOU EVER?

Have you ever heard the wind in the trees?
Have you ever heard the sound of bees?
Have you ever heard the moon go ping?
Have you ever heard a pink frog sing?

Have you ever been out to sea?
Have you ever been out for tea?
Have you ever been in a frog race?
Have you ever been up to space?

Have you ever seen a big green man?
Have you ever seen a small dog van?
Have you ever seen a small blind bee?
Have you ever thought you were

>   *Having your tea?*

Maryanne Temblett (12)
Pontarddulais Comprehensive School

SOMEONE'S KNOCKING

Someone came knocking on my small front door.
I listened for more knocking, but there was no more.
I opened my door and I looked around,
But to my surprise nobody was found.
The wolves are howling under the bright yellow moon,
Then there's a voice saying it won't be soon.
The banging and scratching on my big dark door,
Then to my surprise there was no more.
I crept up the stairs in the dark, black house,
There wasn't any noise, not a squeak of a mouse.
The door started creaking, creaking more,
Then to my surprise there was no more.

Jonathan Eynon (13)
Pontarddulais Comprehensive School

WHY MUST I GO TO SCHOOL?

Must I go to school today,
I really don't want to go
Must I go to school today
I'd rather stay at home
I made my way up to the gate
I didn't realise that I was very late
I walked through the classroom door
And my feet were very, very sore.
Must I go to school today
I really don't want to go
Must I go to school today
I'd rather stay at home today
And tomorrow I will have to go to school
Please don't make me go to school today,
I'd rather stay at home
Oh no I've got to go I have to go to school.

Kirsty Howells (12)
Pontarddulais Comprehensive School

THE MOUNTAIN

I love to go up the mountain
and look at the clouds and sky
I walk through grass and heather
and I often wonder why?
Why do the clouds drift so high?
Why is the air so sweet?
Why is the mountain so huge and solemn
And why is it all so neat?

Sarah Carruthers (13)
Pontarddulais Comprehensive School

My Dream

I had a dream last night,
It happened in the middle of the night,
It had monkeys, elephants, loads of things,
Believe it or not there was a hippo which sings,
There was pencil sharpeners too and stuff,
There was a big old teddy bear which was really rough
You could walk on clouds
Do what you like
There was a guardian
Who looked like Bill Syke.
I tried to make my way
He wouldn't even budge
After 1, 2, 3, I gave him a hard nudge
He picked up his cup then put it back down
Guess what happened then
I woke up on the ground
And that was my dream.

Hannah Simpson (11)
Pontarddulais Comprehensive School

So Quiet

It's so, so quiet in my bed.
I listen to the silence and the noises.
I hear a flutter of a bird in flight
And a clutter of a mouse in a fright.
I hear the wind whistling through the trees.
I hear the faint rustle of the oak's leaves.
In the distance I hear a wolf's cry.
Now the wind has begun to die.
It's so, so quiet in my bed.

Kathryn Thomas (12)
Pontarddulais Comprehensive School

My Birthday

My birthday means a lot to me
I just can't sleep at all
Tossing and turning in my bed
I just can't wait to see

Then in the morning I awake
Wondering what's downstairs
Is everything I want behind that door?
Lots of presents and a cake

Ripping all the wrapping paper off
Waiting to see what presents are there
Toys and more toys and money of course
And a load of dust that made be cough

Then all my friends arrive
And we all go down to town
Spending a little money
Oh how lucky I am to be alive

When I got home my mum lit the candles
And everyone sang happy birthday to me
Then I started wrapping my hair round my fingers
And my hair ended up in tangles.

Siobhan Shannon (11)
Pontarddulais Comprehensive School

FEAR - THE PREDATOR

The eternal blackness of fear,
Has scared so many minds,
It's evil, hellish power, enclosing and engulfing the innocent.
Once it begins it never stops, simply lingers in the darkness,
Waiting to enclose, to spread, to destroy, waiting for a cause.

When a cause comes it pounces,
Immersing its prey helplessly in endless darkness,
Strangling its hope with all its dark powers.
Once the hope is gone the mind cannot live,
Turning from sanity to pure madness.

Fear is evil, terrible and painful,
A huge barren cornfield with no one in sight.
It's lonely, dark, treacherous and greedy.
It has no mercy, no feelings, no remorse.
Nothing is safe from its sharp, deadly claws,
Nor can anything protect,
It will never leave, look back or stop,
Fear will always be there.

Michael Williams (13)
Pontarddulais Comprehensive School

FOOD

Food, food, glorious food
Where would we be without it?
Strawberries and cream,
Oh . . . what a dream!

Vegetables and pasta
Chicken and beef
Tomatoes and cucumber
With a lettuce leaf.

Crisps and chocolate
Is so fab
Eaten in moderation
Ain't too bad.

Burger and chips
Fast food galore
Hot dogs and pizzas
We just want more.

Kelly Stilwell (13)
Pontarddulais Comprehensive School

THE SECRET OF THE WIND

I wondered lonely through the trees,
A swipe of gentle whistling breeze,
Brushed across my freckled face,
Whispered, requesting to have a race,
I jogged, then ran across the land.
The moonlight lightened up the sand,
I came to the sea and was about to end,
Then the wind lifted me to ascend.
Flying, gliding about the sky,
Swooping, swaying here I fly.
Gazing down upon the sea,
Let me fly forever I plead.
This seems like a dream, I've gone so far!
Tell me wind where we are?
You are in a dream, I have captured your heart
Not much longer and we shall be apart.

Emma Bolt (12)
Pontarddulais Comprehensive School

PHEW!

I arrived at school it was my first day
went to my form room

Took a deep breath
Took a look in my bag
Have I got this?
Have I got that?
Am I already for my first class?

I imagined last night
It's just like a test
You've just gotto pass
And try your best
Then make friends with the class.

It was time for lunch
We had to line up
The queue was massive
Year Seven were last
And so I got lost
I see my class
And I finally got to my class
Phew!

Kirsty Wilson (11)
Pontarddulais Comprehensive School

FOOTBALL CRAZY

I know somebody who is a football freak
He plays football every day of the week
I know somebody whose favourite team is Man Utd
Every time they win he gets excited

I know somebody who wants to be a football star
If he keeps practising he will go far
On the field he's as fast as can be
I know somebody who you really should see

I know somebody who runs all over the pitch
Kicking, passing, shooting, it's no hitch
I know somebody who dribbles the ball
Got to be careful, watch out for that wall

I know somebody who trains all the time
Doesn't matter what day, come rain or shine
He football mad and I tell no lies
I know somebody who really tries

Football really is the best
I know somebody who puts it to the test
I know somebody you should see
And that somebody is me.

Richard Thomas Masurier (11)
Pontarddulais Comprehensive School

A World Without Love

Time and time again I dream of
A world full of hatred
A world without love
The world as we know it now

There are no seeds to grow
For the flowers are dead
Nature is dead
Leaves are rotting
The trees have fallen
And all because people
Have stopped caring!
They just kept thinking
Of themselves and starting wars.

Now the world is dead
As we'll be soon
We need to care more
Love one another
Like sister and brother
We might just kill the earth
And we'll kill each other
We must start caring now!

Sarah Westron (11)
Pontarddulais Comprehensive School

I ONCE KNEW A MAN WHO COULD

I once knew a man who could:
Understand a lot about art
And who dressed very smart
And enjoyed a game of darts.

I once knew a man who could:
Balance a brush on his chin
And would you believe it fell in a bin
And cut himself upon a tin.

I once knew a man who could:
Run for at least a mile
Who always kept his style
And never lost his smile.

I once knew a man who could:
Twist and turn his knee
Climb a 50 foot tree
And would you believe it, swim the sea.

I once knew a man who could:
Do a brilliant dance
And his big secret was ants in his pants
I once knew a man!

Emma Thomas (11)
Pontarddulais Comprehensive School

THE DOUBLE LIFE OF A CAT

At the stroke of midnight,
There's something on the streets,
Terrorising mice and rats,
Making them run away in fleets.

But by the time of morning,
A cute cat's in the house,
So smart and very tame,
The monster's gone, peace for a mouse.

But by the middle of the night,
The monster's back you see,
Savagely slaughtering all small life,
Attacking with cruelty.

But by the morning it becomes,
A wonderful companion,
Sitting there by the garden gate,
Purring in the sun.

In the night the demon awakes,
With bloodshot eyes and looking,
A snarl comes from its deep dark mouth,
When it finds a victim lurking.

So you see cats live a double life,
When it's good, evil's in its head,
So on a dark and mysterious night,
Make sure you stay safe in your bed!

Tom Bradshaw (12)
Pontarddulais Comprehensive School

THE OTHER WORLD

The other world
What is it like?
Could it have robots.
And skeletons named Spike?

The people could be aliens,
All dressed in green,
With walking televisions,
Who are mean machines!

Talking dogs could live in spaceships,
Aliens could live in purple trees,
Apples could fly around,
Like bright buzzy bees.

Pineapples could do cartwheels,
Flowers could sing,
The alien that lived in the red tree,
Could be the other world's king.

Birds could swim in the water,
Fish could fly in the air,
Food could jump around,
Even a juicy pear!

So could it be like this,
All weird and swirled,
What would it really be like,
In the other world?

Nia Jermin (12)
Pontarddulais Comprehensive School

LITTLE SUSIE, POOR LITTLE SUSIE

Little Susie, poor little Susie
Wherever she went
Skipping along, teddy bear in her hand and a smile
Upon her face still fell head over heels.

Little Susie, poor little Susie
Wherever she went
She'd trip over laces, slippers, bags and even teddy
And fell head over heels.

Little Susie, poor little Susie,
Wherever she went
The others would cough at her little problem
Yet she still fell head over heels.

Little Susie, poor little Susie
Wherever she went
She'd cry, nursing her cuts and bruises
From falling head over heels.

Little Susie, poor little Susie
Wherever she went
The boys would stop and stare and soon it would be
They who fell head over heels
In love!

Julie Anthony (11)
Pontarddulais Comprehensive School

I Have A Little Brother

I have a little brother
His name is Tommy Joe
I took him to the farmyard
To let him have a go

'A go of what?' you ask him
To which he quickly replied
'I'm off to find a donkey
On which to have a ride'

He wandered round the farmyard
Through the icy snow
Not knowing which direction
He really ought to go

Then out of the crisp cool air
There came a familiar sound
The pounding and the thumping
Of hooves upon the ground

Little Tommy Joe jumped
Up and down with glee
Clapping his hands and
Shouting they've come
Just to see me.

Rachel Williams (11)
Pontarddulais Comprehensive School

A LITTLE BOAT IN A STORMY SEA

The sky was grey, the sea was dark,
Waves were all around and risin',
They broke against the side of the boat,
And all the foam was flyin'.

The boat rocked to 'n' fro,
With all its ropes alashin',
Then the storm broke with all its might,
Lightnin' was aflashin'.

The poor boat pulled at its ropes,
It suddenly broke it's moorin',
It sailed away over the waves,
With nobody drivin'.

The capt'n was asleep below,
Unaware his boat was sailin',
A giant waves rocked the boat,
And sent a mug a flyin'.

The capt'n awoke with a jolt,
He rushed on deck to save himself from dyin',
But to his horror he discovered,
His boat was already divin'.

Robert Barnes (11)
Pontarddulais Comprehensive School

WALKING THROUGH THE FOREST

Walking through the forest
With no care
The wind is blowing
Through my hair.

Walking through the forest
Sun up high
It's shining in my eye
While floating by.

Walking through the forest
On my own
When I tripped
Over a stone.

Walking through the forest
Time is passing by
It's gone really quick
Time does fly.

Walking through the forest
It's getting dark
I looked into the sky
And saw a golden lark.

Sara Lloyd (12)
Pontarddulais Comprehensive School

THE MEANING OF COLOUR!

Colours, colours all around,
Mountain high on the ground,
Full of meaning and stories as well,
Colours are lifelike as I'm about to tell,
Blue is the colour of mysteries,
Black is the colour of dirty fleas,
Red is the colour of romantic days,
Yellow means sweet smelling hay,
Green is the colour of sticky slime,
Brown is the colour of spooky times,
Orange means a blazing fire,
Striking up higher and higher,
Pink is the colour of human flesh,
Purple is the colour of a pretty dress,
White is silent and very plain,
Grey is the colour of nasty rain,
Colours are different in every way,
Some mean happy or grumpy days,
Colours now mean more to me,
They brighten up my heart you see.

Emily Dawson (12)
Pontarddulais Comprehensive School

FOOTBALL NOWADAYS

Football used to be about playing a good game,
But now it's all about your togs' name,
We all like to wear the gear we like,
At the moment mine is Nike.

Each and every day when I wake up,
I've dreamt about winning the FA cup,
I hope one day my dream will come true,
But, until then the dream will do.

I've watched my favourites like Michael Owen,
To be like him I'll have to keep going,
His partner Fowler is brilliant too,
Together they'll show the opposition what they can do.

Each week I train as hard as I can,
Man would I love to play with Zinadine Zidane,
His international team is France,
He takes on players like they're in a trance.

Lee Harris (13)
Pontarddulais Comprehensive School

LOVE

It was a warm September morning when I saw
her there,
Standing in the sunlight with her long golden
hair.
I felt a lovely feeling as though I'd
caught a dove,
It was a happy feeling, I knew that it
was love.

I longed to go and talk to her, my
heart said go ahead,
But my legs were still and would
not move,
Like I was weighed down with
lead.

Love is such a simple thing,
Enjoy it while you can.
For if you ever lose it,
You might not be a man.

Mathew Fuge (12)
Pontarddulais Comprehensive School

MY HOUSE

Welcome to my house
Full of many interesting things
No house like my house
And we get treated like kings

Into the kitchen we all stroll
Watch out for that . . !
Old sausage roll

Next is the living room
The finest of all
But you shouldn't sit there!
Or you'll scratch the wall

That's my sister's bedroom I point out
But don't go in there!
Or you'll get a clout

This is my mum's room
The biggest in the house
You know, my mum is so strange
She's got a pet mouse!

Last but not least
We come to my room
Do you know the difference?
I do . . .
The mess

Dario Fisher (12)
Pontarddulais Comprehensive School

MY LOVE FOR THE WELSH COUNTRY

As I came out on to Wembley
As the crowd roared loud with glee,
Proud to wear the big red shirt
I was as happy as can be.
Happy, shouting as 'Number 1,' went in
Then they came back with three.
I didn't know what happened
The ref had blown for a penalty.
Jason Price stepped up to take it
I was as happy as can be
As I rounded one, stepped past another
The ball left my feet and across went another.
Down went Glen Hoddle,
'What's happened to my team?'
Three all after extra time it was penalties.
The Welsh went first, *bang* we scored
Then it was me.
I focused myself bottom right
I started to run
Then the ball moved
Wide it flew, my head sunk.
The ref blew his whistle, 'Take it again.'
The Welsh had won the trophy
I had scored the winning goal.
Bzzz! Went the buzzer.
'Home time' said the English teacher.

Thomas Millard (13)
Pontarddulais Comprehensive School

AUTUMNAL FALL

Autumn is like a rich multicoloured coat,
Reds, yellows and browns are the hues of note.

Autumn's dew will cover the grass,
And summer's days are long, long past.

Leaves are falling from the trees,
With the cold but gentle breeze.

All across the silvery lake,
Shadows dance and twist and shake.

Hedgehogs scurry across the ground,
Eating the insects they have found.

Squirrels scamper through the trees,
Searching for nuts with apparent ease.

Birds peck at autumn's cold berries,
They are the last of summer's bright red cherries.

Michaelmas daisies will soon be gone,
As the birds sing their last summer song.

Autumn's marigolds will finally disappear,
With the first sign of winter's frosty atmosphere.

The farmer's busy in his fields,
Gathering crops that earth yields.

Silvery stars dance in the night,
With the last of summer's delight.

Frosty weather is to come,
Fingers and toes will soon be numb!

Aimee Richards (12)
Pontarddulais Comprehensive School

MY CAT . . . WAFFLES!

My cat Waffles, aaah . . .! What a stupid thing
He struts around the house
As if he's a king.

His tail all wiggly and up in the air,
He's guaranteed to give cats
One heck of a scare.

In the winter when it is all cold and wet
He curls up to you and purrs
Just like a purr. . . fect pet.

He slurps his milk until it's all gone
He then starts to miaow
Which sounds just like a song.

He plays in the garden with a little ball,
He starts to miaow
As if it's some sort of call.

If Ginger cat comes in the house
Old wise Waffle always
Chases it out like a mouse.

Oh well he's gone to sleep
I can't resist it
I have to have a peak.

He looks so peaceful all there by himself,
Unlike the time
When he fell off the shelf.

All we can hear throughout the house
Is his quiet purr . . . purr . . .
purr . . . purr . . .

Michael Thomas (13)
Pontarddulais Comprehensive School

ROUNDERS TEAM

Positions, positions
Get to your positions
The game of rounders is about to begin.

Bowling, bowling,
I'm first in bowling
Watch out, opponents, we're going to win.

Now run, first base is falling,
Look she's scoring
Oh this is boring!
What's the score?
Twenty four.

Hit the ball with the bat
Not your hat
What's the score?
Thirty four.

Change teams,
Get to your positions
The next game of rounders is about to begin.

Bowling, bowing
I'm first bowling
Watch out again we're going to win.

Jasmine Kelly (12)
Pontarddulais Comprehensive School

MANIACS

Maniacs have cruel minds,
They always blow a fuse.
And when people come near them
They give 'em a big fat bruise.

I've seen it once,
In the hall,
When I was big,
No, I think I was small.

He charged through,
Like a big stone brick.
With his big bulky head,
Which was quite thick.

Everyone moved,
As they heard him coming,
But those who didn't
Got a very big thumping.

Nobody goes near,
Anyone who's mad,
Because every one knows,
They'll be kicked in pretty bad.

Alan Evans (13)
Pontarddulais Comprehensive School

SAVE THE WHALES

The right, humpback and blue whales
Are all endangered species
As they fight for the right to live.

The grey, sperm and fin whales
Are all quite vulnerable
As they try to survive in the wild.

The blue whale is a prime target
Because of its great size at 26 meters
Compared to us its a giant!

The whalers kill them
For their meat and blubber
Which is really very mean.

Now that Kako the whale is free
She can live a life in the sea
In a world of freedom and peace.

Greenpeace try I am sure
To stop the killers and captors
But they can't always be there to save them.

The results of Greenpeace studies
Can provide a clearer view
Of the plight of whales.

Cheryl Scott (13)
Pontarddulais Comprehensive School

My Cat!

My little cat
There she lies
Shiny coat
Bright green eyes.

Whiskers long
Ears stood up
Alert she is
That's my cat!

Good as she looks
Naughty she is
Nooks she will find
But I don't mind.

She's my cat
A little ball of fur
Her tongue is rough
But that is her.

A friend she is
She follows me around
Tammy's her name
I hope it's now clear!

That's my cat!

Jenna Griffiths (13)
Pontarddulais Comprehensive School

MY GRAN

My gran is very caring
My gran is kind and warm
And each and every Saturday
I help her mow her lawn.

My gran is very helpful,
My gran is very funny
And for her 50th birthday
I bought her a little white bunny.

My gran puts up with my grandad
My gran puts up with my mum
And between my mum and my grandad
No wonder she looks so glum.

My gran does a lot of work
My gran does it all in the house
So it is very, very surprising
That she is as quiet as a mouse.

My gran is the best
My gran doesn't need a test
Because as long as I like her as she is,
She will always beat the rest.

Luke Raddenbury (13)
Pontarddulais Comprehensive School

AZURE BLUE

I wonder what life is like,
At the bottom of the sea
At the deepest, darkest, part of all
Is there life there yet to see?

Creepy crawlies, monsters too
Giant squid and whales that cry
Roam the seas of azure blue
Floating in their watery sky.

How do they speak, what do they say
What do the dolphins do
Is it just swimming, eating and playing
In the seas of azure blue.

Have you every seen anything so ridiculous
As a seahorse swimming by
But what could be more terrifying
Than a shark giving you his evil eye.

Slippery seaweed of green and brown
Tentacled anemones waving by
Crunchy crabs and lobsters too
Live in their liquid azure sky.

Stewart Edwards (14)
Pontarddulais Comprehensive School

EXCUSES

My margin's gone all crooked Miss
My ruler's broke in half
My work blew out the window Miss
My cow gave birth to a calf
I wrote on the wrong page Miss
My book was upside down
Every time I see you Miss
I always wear a frown
My pencil went all blunt Miss
My book was back to front
The leg fell off my chair Miss
My dog ate my work
My arm broke in half Miss
My auntie had a coughing fit
My uncle had a new car
My cousin went too far Miss
My sister was a star
Yes I'll do it again Miss
In my dinnertime.

Gemma Coffey (13)
Pontarddulais Comprehensive School

WHERE'S THE PEACE?

A world filled with war
A world full of guns
A world full of fear
A world without fun
A world where innocent people are killed.

A heart full of anger
A heart full of fright
A heart full of fear
A heart without fun
A heart which is helpless to stop the carnage.

A mind full of emptiness
A mind without life
A mind full of fear
A mind without fun
A mind with no understanding of why this goes on.

Where's the peace?

Laura Kaltenbach (14)
Pontarddulais Comprehensive School

SLY AS A FOX

Slowly and slyly
He crept through the wild
Dark, damp, barbarous woods
With only one thing on his mind
Stealthily he pondered
Licking his lips
The woods are alive, mysterious and bewitched
But he is cunning, cognisant and cautious
He is planning every move to the last detail
He is very focused
Wise
And inclined.
He suddenly leaps over the farmer's gate
Edging ever closer to his prey
He hasn't eaten in days
He has been lingering
Looking for a chance like this for days . . .
He must not fail!
Quietly he started pacing towards his catch
Staying vigilant at all times . . .
Just in case of a farmer!
Or dog!
He bounced onto the ledge
Leading up to the old, rotted, bashed, disintegrating barn
It was a chicken barn . . .
Steadily he approached the small door . . .
He entered . . . !

Dale Thomas (13)
Pontarddulais Comprehensive School

Mum

I want a dog,
I want a cat,
I want a budgie or two.
I want a hippo,
I want a lion,
Or give me a kangaroo.

I want a car,
I want a bike,
I want a TV with legs.
I want a bag,
I want a tent,
With shiny silver pegs.

I want a pen,
I want a ruler,
I want a six-foot pencil case.
I want a sharpener,
I want a rubber,
I want a new make-up set for my face.

I want new shoes,
I want new clothes,
I want a millionaire for a mother.
I want a hat,
I want a boat,
But Mum,
I don't want a
Baby brother!

Kirsty Evans (12)
Pontarddulais Comprehensive School

SCHOOL DINNERS

S is for sandwiches, squash and sausages.
C is for chips and cakes.
H is for hungry children.
O is for oranges.
O is for onions.
L is for lunch.

D is for dinner ladies.
I is for icing on top of the cakes.
N is for nutrition.
N is for nourishment.
E is for eating the scrumptious food.
R is for rolls.
S is for school dinners.

A is for apple juice.
R is for roast potatoes
E is for delicious eclairs.

G is for garlic bread.
R is for red tomatoes.
E is for empty stomachs if you don't eat food.
A is for apples
T is for tummy which is full of food!

Joanne Richards (12)
Pontarddulais Comprehensive School

WACKY ANIMALS

Imagine an elephant,
Sweet and cuddly.
Imagine a kitten,
Fat and ugly.

Imagine a hippo,
With spots.
Imagine a crocodile,
With dreadlocks.

Imagine a bee,
Without its stripes.
Imagine a lion,
Without its fierce bites.

Imagine a polar bear,
Without its coat.
Imagine a giraffe,
Being very short.

Imagine a world,
So weird and wild.
Strange but true,
Without mankind.

Amber Carlisle (12)
Pontarddulais Comprehensive School

HEN HOUSE

Slowly and surely
but yet very
fox-like
It's like looking for X
Where the chicken lies awaiting him
He creeps through
the dark,
damp, dull forest.
As he exits the woods
It's there! The hen house!
He creeps up on all four legs
making sure that the farmer doesn't even
see him.
He gets there,
digs at an horrendous speed
gets under the wire
to the hen house
with only one thing on his mind.
Hoping the farmer doesn't even see him,
he says slyly,
'Three seconds and counting
three, two, one'
attack!
The chickens scatter in all directions
he grabs one,
runs over the fields.
The farmer shoots but misses
and he is safe with food.

James Mainwaring (12)
Pontarddulais Comprehensive School

Sports

Sports, all kinds of them.
Football, rugby, racing, swimming
To some even gambling's a sport,
Not me, I'm too young for that
But sports how I love them,
All kinds of them.

Athletics, gym, running and javelin.
Very . . . Olympic those.
Long jump, triple jump,
I only thought that there was one sort of jump.
But sports how I love them,
All kinds of them.

Long distances, short distances,
Runners having to run miles.
I'll take a car for those.
And how quick have you got to be on those short distances?
Very quick!
But sports how I love them,
All kinds of them.

All of these sports,
Or well most are played with balls
Why aren't balls square?
They'd still be soft enough to use
It's all so confusing,
But sports how I love them,
Every single one of them.

Leon Thyer (13)
Pontarddulais Comprehensive School

ICE!

Cold,
Biting,
Bitter,
Bleak,
Chilled,
Chilly,
Freezing freak,

Hostile,
Frosty,
Frigid,
Iciness,
Frozen,
Shivery,
Distant,
Frostiness,

Harden,
Stiffen,
Glacial,
Numbing,
Penetrating,
Wintry,
Arctic,
Cutting!

Simone Morris (12)
Pontarddulais Comprehensive School

SITTING ON A PILE OF GOLD

A dragon awoke
After a
Thousand years' sleep.
Sitting on his
Pile of gold.
Treasures
Forgotten
Never seen
Not known.
A dragon
Sitting all alone
Lonesome
Forlorn
An abandoned myth
Unknown to the outside world.
Sitting under a mountain of people
Alone in the civilised world.
People walking around
Oblivious to the dragon below
Blinded by their lifestyle.
Under their roads lives a dragon
Completely forgotten
Living alone.

Kaity Lee (12)
Pontarddulais Comprehensive School

Marble Girl

The girl
In the middle of the room
A big, dark, echoing room
So frightened but calm
So loud-speaking but so soft
With modern-day clothes
Wandering around
In an old-fashioned building
Crumbling down
She disappears into the light
Where has she gone?
What does she see?
Will she come back?
Or is the light too bright?
She left this marble
I don't know why!
But all I know
If she comes back
She will not stay
I kept this marble to this day
I will always remember her
In my own special way.

Amanda Robertson (12)
Pontarddulais Comprehensive School

IMAGINARY CREATURES

Beasts,
Who like to eat feasts.
They like the night,
But not the light.

Monsters,
They are tall,
And don't like to fall.

Elves,
They can't put up shelves.
They are small,
And they like to play ball.

Unicorns,
They have a big horn,
And they like to eat popcorn.

Dragons,
They like fire,
But they aren't for hire.

Fairy, fairy,
Your clothes are so flairy.
You are so twinkly,
And so wrinkly.

Linda Taylor (12)
Pontarddulais Comprehensive School

ROLLER-COASTER

Going on a trip,
to a theme park ride,
going slow,
going fast,
swaying back,
swaying forward,
loop the loop,
around and around,
everybody's dizzy,
going to the top,
ohhh nooo!
We're going *doownnn!*
Everybody's screaming,
hands up in the air,
here we go!
Loop the loop
on our last climb . . .
Aahh!
Going down really fast!
On the straight - we're slowing down.
At the stop. Everybody's happy,
walking off the ride,
very, very, dizzy.

Michael Evans (12)
Pontarddulais Comprehensive School

BONFIRE NIGHT

Bonfire night,
Crackling fire makes the night glow,
Golden crisp brown colours,
Cold, cold night shivers up your spine,
Smell of hot dogs fills the air,
Fireworks burst into bright luminous colours,
Bang bang! Crash crash!
Coloured ones,
Noisy ones,
Shooting ones,
That never seem to come down,
Dark gloomy shadows,
Breath that clouds in the air,
Bright faces all aglow, thinking, dreaming,
Eyes transfixed on hissing Catherine wheels,
The night draws in,
It's very late,
The fire dies down,
Fireworks fall,
Everyone leaves,
All that's left is the ash of the fire,
Left to burn away.

Alexandra Hawken (12)
Pontarddulais Comprehensive School

THE TIGER

He's big, strong and proud, striding through the night,
With big wide eyes and ever so alert ears, he's on the lookout.
The tall thin reeds rustle in the night.
He stops in his tracks thinking is this my supper?
His ears prick up, his mouth opens wide, he pounces.
There's a struggle, a scream and then silence.
His sharp, bright fangs rip into his latest triumph.
The canines strip the meat from the carcass inch by inch.
His shiny green eyes displaying his delight,
As he eats into his unfortunate victim.
His fangs drip with bright red blood.
The scavengers arrive in hope of a share.
The tiger roars at the top of his voice.
The hyenas take note and scatter.
Having completed his meal,
He gets up and strolls to the river for a liquid refreshment.
He then climbs a tree and stretches over the branches.

Anna Nowak (13)
Pontarddulais Comprehensive School

BOOKS

What are books?
Are they long, short,
fiction or not?
Are they classics or autobiographies?
For young or for old?
Picture books, reading books -
what do you like?
You must like something!
Come on, take your pick!
What sort of books do you like?

Books are a visit to fairyland -
or it could be a trip to the Alps!
With mysteries and adventures,
you could find something just for you.
Finding a book is just like choosing a cake!
You've just got to find the right one.
My friend Aimée likes horse books,
and I like crime,
listen to this message and get into books!

Charlene Smith (12)
Pontarddulais Comprehensive School

TIME

Time,
Time governs life,
Whether or not we want it to,
We cannot change it,
Slow it down,
Or increase its pace,
It has always been here,
It will stay here forever,
Time,
It depends on our waking up in the morning,
Missing or catching a bus,
We see it everywhere,
Television,
Oven clocks,
Standing in a busy city,
It goes on night and day,
Whatever the weather,
All over the world,
Time.

Sarah Price (12)
Pontarddulais Comprehensive School

TREES HIGH IN THE SKY

The tree is a plant,
Which grows very high,
Its leaf-covered branches
Reach out to the sky.
There's sycamore, cedar
Oak and the yew,
There's so many species
I could only name a few.

                        Deciduous trees shed
                        Their leaves in winter
                        But the evergreens seem
                        To go on forever.
                        The wood from trees
                        Has hundreds of uses
                        From furniture-making
                        To the building of houses.

Longbows for archers
Were made from the yew,
But the willow to me
Rules over all,
Without it there'd be no bat
To hit the cricket ball.

Gemma Evans (12)
Pontarddulais Comprehensive School

SANTA CLAUS

On a cold cold night when the snow was fresh and my nose
was strawberry red,
I was told a tale of a dear old man who flew around in a sled,
'A sled' said I to my baffled mum who sat by the fake fir-tree,
'He rides through the sky on this magical night with presents
for you and me' said she,
'He lives in the north where the animals talk and his belly
wobbles like jelly,
With his candycorn house, he's as gentle as a mouse,
and he's always jolly and merry.
His long white beard grows down to the ground
and his elves with their long pointy ears dance around,
And all in one night around the world he goes
led by Rudolph and his red shiny nose.
And we hang our stockings on the end of our bed
with excitement in our eyes we nod our tiny heads.
He knows if we've been good or bad,
will we get coal or something else?
And in the morning we wake to find treasures
and goodies of every kind,'
Their faces filled with joy and glee
sit and play under the Christmas tree.
'Aren't you curious' she said to me 'who this man may be?'
'It's Santa Claus' I said to her 'daddy told me last week!'

Gemma Roberts (13)
Pontarddulais Comprehensive School

SUNDAYS

Sundays I hate,
Homework left late,
Sunday's lunch,
Turns out to be brunch,
Because I got up so late.
Grampa snoozing,
But not from boozing,
He's trying to escape,
The washing of the plates,
Sundays!

My sister Alys,
Full of malice,
Shouting in my ear,
Dad is ignoring,
The Grand Prix his calling,
Sundays!

Sunday family tea,
It's not for me,
Shall we go for a walk,
Or sit around and talk?
I flee to my room,
Plague with my music
Boom, boom, boom,
Sundays!

The day nearly done,
With 'All Saints' number one,
Homework still not completed,
Sunday night gloom,
My music still booms,
Monday looms,
Lights out,
Who needs Sundays!

Sarah Worthing (13)
Pontarddulais Comprehensive School

MY TOWN SWANSEA

Swansea is the place to be
Hip, hop, and happening,
Come to Ritzy!

Castle Gardens is the place to hang
Wearing baggy pants,
And blading if they can.

HMV with the happy sounds,
The CDs normally cost a couple of pounds.

Joe's ice-cream is so delish,
There's so many different flavours,
Coffee-nut is my favourite dish.

Café Mambo is the place to eat,
Lamb cutlets with mint sauce,
It goes down like a treat.

Pubs and clubs are for older teens,
Come in your best outfit,
(That doesn't mean jeans).

The UCI which shows all the top films,
Popcorn and nachos,
Live out your dreams.

Swimming about in Swansea Leisure,
Tennis, ice-skating and parties,
Gives us a lot of pleasure.

That's what's happening in groovy town,
So invite all your mates to come and see,
Swansea is the place to be!

Vanessa Moyes (14)
Pontarddulais Comprehensive School

OLD AGE

45 and fat, middle age has certainly arrived
My descent into this decrepit state can no longer be denied.

Bags under eyes, bloated face and double chin,
A fight against time I was destined never to win.

Midlife crisis, new job, a divorce,
To get out of bed in the morning myself I have to force.

Blood pressure, heart attacks, endless ills,
Your doctor recommending new vitamin pills.

Retirement looming just ahead,
What to do in the day after I rise from my bed?

Christmas time all alone,
Longing for the kids to phone.

Schooldays were the best of my life,
Then I never knew the meaning of trouble and strife.

Oh well, there's always retirement, yes it may be great,
I just have to come to terms with this new-found elderly state.

Caroline Jones (13)
Pontarddulais Comprehensive School

SEASONS

Autumn leaves are falling all around
They fall so lightly they don't make a sound
Some are brown and some are red
But in spring they are green instead
Children playing in the park
They run around as the dogs bark
But then winter settles in
Everything is white, cold and grim
The park is empty the children are gone
Everyone stays at home where it's warm
Most kinds of flowers are long since dead
And children tell tales of a man dressed in red
When spring comes along there's a sign of new life
The snow is all gone and the children fly kites
Eggs are hatching in the nest
Robins and blue tits are the ones I like best
Then there is summer it's nice and it's warm
Families go down to the beach and there's ice-cream all around
Children are swimming in the sea
Lots of fun for you and me
Oh but which season is best I hear you say
They are all very special in their own special way.

Sarah Gwenter (13)
Pontarddulais Comprehensive School

SKATING IN THE PARK!

I like skating it gives me a buzz
I don't know why
But it just does

I like skating in the park
Skating around in the dark
I go grinding on the kerbs
And when I fall it really hurts

I go skating when it's damp
Doing fakie 540s over the ramp
When I grind I do a Soul
All the way
Down the pole

I play street hockey with my friends
Once we start playing the fun never ends

I love blading
It is such fun
Even though I fall on my bum

Every day when I go out
I go blading without a doubt.

Daniel Carlisle (13)
Pontarddulais Comprehensive School

SPACE

There are nine planets in the sky
The sun and moon and stars
Rockets fly up in the air
To planets such as Mars.

Are there Martians out there
ETs, aliens too
I don't know just what to say
Is it just untrue?

Is anybody out there
A man inside the moon
Since man has been exploring
We'll find out pretty soon.

Armstrong landed on the moon
Guess just what he found?
Dust and rock and craters
Scattered on the ground.

I'd like to fly a rocket
Far out into space
One step just for mankind
And for the human race.

Vaughan O'Neill (13)
Pontarddulais Comprehensive School

School

I wouldn't say school is cool
With all the lessons that we have
And all the homework we have to do
Given by teachers in our school

With learning French I could go to France
With learning German I could go to Germany
What a great opportunity

There is maths that I don't like
But it could be helpful in the future
And then IT
To show me how
To use a computer

I enjoy doing drama
Acting on stage is a lot of fun
Breaking the drama rules would be rather dumb
Don't goldfish and don't turn your back
If you don't break the rules
You will have a huge big clap

Music is fun
Playing the glockenspiel
And learning to sing and reading music

Don't you think school is cool?

Beverley Taylor (13)
Pontarddulais Comprehensive School

ICE-CREAM

Ice-cream is my favourite food,
I can eat it whatever my mood.
With lots of flavours which are cool,
If you don't like them you must be a fool.

Toffee, fudge, or chocolate chip
Or tutti-fruiti take your pick.
If you can't decide because they're all
so neat
mix and match and you'll have a treat.

Carte d'or is my favourite kind
Or Hagen Daas I don't mind.
There are loads of toppings which are
great,
Why not share some with your mate?

I eat more ice-cream when it's hot,
It really cools me down a lot.
When I'm older I'm going to
Make lots more ice-cream for me and
you.

I'll get fatter and burst one day,
I don't care, at least I can say
'I've eaten every flavour ice-cream,
Aren't I the luckiest girl ever seen?'

Faye Chatfield (13)
Pontarddulais Comprehensive School

MUSIC!

Banging on the drums
Singing into the mic
It's as easy as riding a bike

Blowing into the trumpet
Plucking the strings
Violins - what noisy things

I want to be famous
I'd like to be the best
But for today I'll give it a rest
I'll be back tomorrow
To play my music
That's if I'm not sick

I'm going to teach my brother
And maybe my mother
I don't know how
But I'll try them out
And give them a go of . . .

Banging on the drums
Singing into the mic
After all
It's as easy as riding a bike.

Stacie Ellison (13)
Pontarddulais Comprehensive School

FANTASY IN FAIRYLAND

If you see some magic seeds,
In a field of grass,
Very lightly step around,
Creep softly as you pass.

If you find tiny seeds,
Growing where they lie,
Shut your eyes and run away
Be sure that you don't spy.

When the tiny magic seeds,
Grow into golden bells,
Be careful that you tell no one
Or you'll break a magic spell.

Around those little golden bells,
Will form a fairy ring,
In a magic fantasy dell
Full of spangly fluttering wings.

Oh! to dance in fairyland
To float in a golden lagoon,
With frolicking urchins hand in hand
All under a shining silver moon.

Sarah Whitehead (13)
Pontarddulais Comprehensive School

A Friend Is!

A friend is someone who's always there
Armed with a smile and a listening ear,
Mending patches of a broken heart,
Ending rumours before they start.

A friend is someone without a frown,
Spreading happiness all around,
A friend is someone who helps you along,
Keeps you happy and makes you strong.

A call from a friend when you're feeling sad,
Cheers you up and makes you glad,
It's nice to know she's always there,
So that we may always care.

When my friend walks by my side,
Walking in a happy stride,
She brightens up the world around me,
Showing that she really loves me.

Friendship is a priceless gift,
That can't be bought or sold,
Having an understanding friend,
Is worth far more than gold!

Gabrielle Thomas (13)
Pontarddulais Comprehensive School

OUCH!

I've just been bombed by a bumblebee,
Stung by a wasp on my nose,
Attacked in the sea by a jellyfish,
Got broken glass between my toes.

When my auntie's dog, whose name is Jock,
The sneaky little scruff,
Bit me when I patted him,
I'd really had enough!

When I got home to eat my tea,
I burnt my tongue on a faggot
And the salad I ate wasn't too great,
In fact I swallowed a maggot!

As I sat down in my comfy chair,
After my sickening tea,
The electrics in my house went *bang!*
And blew up my TV.

Today was not the best of days,
In fact I feel half-dead,
And if it's the same tomorrow
I'm going back to bed!

Louise David (13)
Pontarddulais Comprehensive School

THE TIGER

With orange fur and dark black stripes,
He roams the forest through the night.
His bright shining eyes and long sharp teeth,
Looking for something tasty to eat.

His huge paws, creep so quietly over the forest floor,
Waiting, waiting.

Shhh! a movement,
Ready to pounce,
He makes his kill.

All night he feasts away and all the left over
                                he saves for day.

He sleeps the day except a while when,
he eats away.

Ceri Gazey (13)
Pontarddulais Comprehensive School

THE ARTIST

There I am sitting in my chair
With my paints beside me.
I look out of my window
And I see a blue tit, in a tree.
I put my paintbrush in my brown for that huge trunk.

Then I see a squirrel run up the trunk
And pick an acorn.
I get some blue and a little white
I start to paint the sky.
There it is a masterpiece
Only if a real artist could see.

I take another sheet to paint the perfect barn
An owl browner than brown.
A rat family running around
Mam, Dad and three little ones.
Here comes big farmer
With his big gun, *bang, bang, bang* it goes.
He blows a bird down.
Everything runs for cover.

Daniel Kelly (12)
Pontarddulais Comprehensive School

BLADING

Every day straight after school
I rush straight home, as a rule
Off go my shoes, on my eyes go my shades
And straight on my feet go my Rhino blades
Away then I go - I'm back after dark
Off with my pals to skate in the park
My pals are called Vaughan, the other is Rob
We skate all the evening - a difficult job
But while we are skating, keeping fast pace
My mind is all wandering to a faraway place
I'm skiing in Canada or on a hill in Peru
If it will make you happy you can come too
We'll go up very slowly, come down very fast
I can go first, and you can go last
Sometimes when I'm blading I slip and I fall
Sometimes I can't stop and bump into a wall
My blades are terrific, the wheels are the best
They glide along smoothly - I don't need a rest
So if you would like to soar like a lark
Come with me blading up to the park.

David Borthwick (13)
Pontarddulais Comprehensive School

MY BEST FRIEND

There's a girl in my class
Her name's Jenny McMillan,
And everyone knows
She's a bit of a villain

My mum doesn't like her
Nor does my dad,
They say she's a hooligan
And this drives me mad

Okay, so she's scruffy
And hopeless at school,
But that doesn't mean she's
An absolute fool

She's brilliant at skipping
And juggling with balls,
And no one can beat her
At climbing up walls

She's my best friend
And I think she's fine
You can choose your friends
And I can choose mine.

Rhian Arrowsmith (14)
Pontarddulais Comprehensive School

What A Dream

The night was dark,
The valley was empty,
Silence in the air,
Spirits were crawling,
Crackling all the leaves,
Laying upon the ground,
My heart beat,
Thud, thud,
There is goes,
When will this nightmare end?
Sweat trickling down my face,
Hands sweaty and wet,
My mind telling me to run, run away,
My heart telling me to stay and see,
What it is, go on have a look,
Before I knew it I was running,
Harder than I had ever run before,
Run, run, run away,
Then I heard a voice,
A familiar voice,
It said,
'Wake up John, wake up, it's only a dream!'

Rebecca Chapman (13)
Pontarddulais Comprehensive School

ANGER

What's anger?
What's it all about?
Is it just one of your emotions,
That makes you want to shout?
It burns up inside you,
Just waiting to break free,
Suddenly it bursts out,
Is this what anger's all about?

What's anger?
What's it all about?
Is it the bad side of people,
When you're in a pout.
Anger takes over,
You just want to scream,
Are you gonna fight the urge
Or are you just gonna be mean?

What's anger?
What's it all about?
Is it when someone does wrong,
And you just let your feelings out?
You turn red with anger,
Sweat runs down your face,
Then sooner or later,
You're yelling down the place.
Is this what anger's all about?

Samantha Mogford (12)
Pontarddulais Comprehensive School

VULTURES

The photos you took and the people that looked
like magpies just wanting a glimpse of gold
scavenging like vultures cruel and cold.

The flashing and prying, the hurt that you caused
photographers blinded by their own money thirst
you crashed the car with your stupid outbursts.

They stepped on the gas to escape the nations' curiosity
and reached such a high velocity in a flash of black they
entered the light to a place where they couldn't be hounded
out of sight.

Take the money from your pockets and glimpse the gold
you could say that's why she died, but it's not true
she died for everyone of us a love she showed so bold.

She gave us her heart and the most beautiful smile
she had the most wonderful aura, but fatefully died
just remember as she did, a smile's for free and so
is the love that she gave to thee.

A princess of people and hearts, she'll always be
please feel the sorrow that you've felt today and learn
from this lesson the feeling of pain.

Walk down the street and smile as you go, give love to each other
as she did so. She hasn't gone, her spirit will always
live on, she gave us everything and asked for nothing
but she's left us with a lesson and everything to learn.

William Bootyman (13)
Pontarddulais Comprehensive School

The Knight

Upon his steed of the purest white,
Sat a tall dark figure, a shining knight,
All dressed in black with lance and shield,
A mace and chain all ready to wield.
No look of fear in his cold hard eyes,
As he raised his head to the clear blue skies,
And utters a prayer to the God he trusts,
And into the horses flanks his spurs he thrusts,
His charger moves forward at an easy pace,
He's in no hurry to meet his enemy's face.
Onward, onward, they gather speed.
There's no turning back it's win or bleed,
At full gallop the knight comes around
With shield held tight and lance bearing down,
He charges his enemy with all his might.
A bloody battle a deadly fight,
And whose fate shall be sealed.
A bloodied knight a battered shield,
One warrior lives and one lies dead,
But the victor's head is as heavy as lead
As he salutes an adversary as brave as he
And thinks to himself that could have been me.

James Beynon (12)
Pontarddulais Comprehensive School

HOUSE GHOST

Airing cupboard ghosts gurgling in the water tank.
Have you heard them?
Bedroom ghosts bang your door in he middle
of the night.
Have you seen them?
Cupboard ghosts pop out in the middle of the night.
Have you seen them?
Landing ghosts creak in the middle of the night.
Have you heard them?
Brothers and sister ghosts beat you up in
the middle of the night.
Have you seen them?
Television ghosts run their fingers across the screen
Have you seen them?
Radiator ghosts click in the night.
Have you heard them?
Light ghosts go on and off in the night.
Have you seen them?
Bathroom ghosts pull you down the toilet
Pull you down the toilet
Pull you down the toilet
       Whoops I've gone!

Scott Thomas (11)
Pontarddulais Comprehensive School

SEASONS

It is unto the river's cry,
That fallest in the raging sky,
Without a doubt it will dry out,
But not until the storm turns drought,

'Twill not be long till the birds' song,
Once more travels through the air,
The nights grow long,
The season's song, shall stay forever there.

'Twill soon be spring,
Great bells shall ring,
As couples tie the knot,
It won't seem long till once again
There's a baby in the cot

With great rejoice the summer comes,
The swallow's back, so too the plums.
The children now do skip and dance,
Their parents watching at a glance.

But once again we'll all get rain,
As Christmas starts to take its strain,
From empty pockets,
Great things are asked,
The shopping now becomes a task,
'Twill be done by those with patience,
They'll not even utter one complaint,
Though this may take some great restraint.

The cycle now once more begins,
Oh God, forgive us for our sins.

Philip Mathias (16)
Pontarddulais Comprehensive School

ACHTUNG! SPITFIRE!

All the men charged to their Spitfires ready to shoot down the Hun,
None of the men were afraid, they were briefed to come out of the sun,
The sky was as clear as their hatred for Hitler, so-called man,
They knew of his barbarities, the Nazis they craved to ban,
The few Churchill called them, the brave for you and me
The young Polish, French and British lads who kept Britannia free,
Up, up, up to the sky the Spitfire flew ready to attach to their score,
Of course, soon pilots they would need more,
Adventure that soon would become a nightmare,
Plus all the people below could do was watch and stare,
Across the passage they flew to meet the Me109
Their orders were clear *'Seek and destroy'* fine
The intruder of their homeland shall go down in flames, full of lead
'Aim for the machines not the man' the CO had said,
They make a dive, they aim steady,
The wing-man shouted 'Ready?'
They pulled the trigger felt the power surge
Everything slowed down as the first bullets emerged
Then the famous cry of *'Achtung! Spitfire!'*
The sound that every German dreads is the British shouting *'Fire'*
One of the most effective aircraft of its time
Before the Yankee's planes came in two for a dime
The most common of pilots had only spent two hours in the
                                                        gallant plane
The only thing that can keep a pilot sane
I hope you can remember these few lads
Who ran the sky (the fathers of your dads)
So don't mock the old, remember what they did
Remember what they did when they were a kid.

Alistair H Veck (12)
Pontarddulais Comprehensive School

Why?

I was wondering yesterday,
Why do boys always fight?
Why do men watch so much sport?
Why are elephants so big?
Why do girls cry so much?
Why do parents always think they're right?
Why are witches' hats always pointed?
Why do people die?
Why are ants so small?
Why do onions make you cry?
Why are some people double jointed?
Why does fluff always come in your belly button?
Why do leaves change colour in autumn?
Why is the sky blue?
Why is the grass green?
Why do dogs sniff each other's butts?
Why do bees buzz?
Why do flies exist?
Why is Tetris so addictive?
Then I thought, why not?

Steven Harrison Dewitt (11)
Pontarddulais Comprehensive School

SPACE FLIGHT

I wait patiently and silently in the huge spacecraft
Sweat rolls down my face like an over-flowing waterfall
10 9 8 7 6 5 4 3 2 1 0 blast off!
Here we are in deep space
I see lots of stars around me blooming
Bursting
It's a hot ball of flaming gas
Coming towards us I'm terrified
My back aches in an uncomfortable position
Then it softly, gently disappears
In the corner of my eye I see the waiting, watching moon
Glistening, glancing, shining, beautifully
In the other corner of my eye
I see the deep dark orange sun
Looking at you blinding you
I turned the spacecraft around with a blurry sight
I see the colours of Mars
I see all different planets beside it
I turned the spacecraft around
I enjoyed my trip in deep space.

Sarah Evans (11)
Pontarddulais Comprehensive School

The Monster

In the mansion I was there
Combing my long brown hair,
Sitting on the stair,
Singing songs of prayer.

I went out to get cough medicine,
I saw some people with a gun
They were the Mafia,
I had to run.

I ran to the house,
And up the stairs,
Some ghosts were playing
Truth or dare.

In my room I saw him
The monster that took my dustbin.
I ran and ran and ran out the door
To find the Mafia that I saw.

They crowded round me
I could not run
They started to take
Out their guns

One man said to me 'My name is Peter,'
And I play the guitar
They took out guitars and violins
And then the monster started to sing . . .

We do the Monster, the Monster Mash
We do the Monster . . .

Cheryl Davies (11)
Pontarddulais Comprehensive School

HOT AIR BALLOON

The roar of the fan,
The heat of the burner,
The shouts of the people below.
As it rises to the skies,
To thousands of cries,
The hot air balloon is on its way.

The retrieve crew follow down below,
Chasing the balloon on its journey.
With the help of maps and a radio,
They follow it on their way.

The balloon lands safely in a farmer's field.
The farmer's as pleased as punch.
The crew go in to pack up the balloon,
They put everything into
The trailer,
Until the next time it flies and takes
To the blue skies of Swansea.

The pilot thanks the farmer as
He and his crew start the journey home.
They all arrive home and unload the gas
Cylinders for refuelling.

The roar of the fan,
The heat of the burner,
The shouts of the people below.
As it rises to the skies,
To thousands of cries,
The hot air balloon is on its way.

Emma Caie (11)
Pontarddulais Comprehensive School

PONTARDDULAIS

I used to live in Manchester
But now I live in Bont
I moved here seven years ago
and this year started comp

I live in Heol-y-Cae
With just fields out the back
When the rain falls from the sky
The clouds they go all black

In Manchester it rains a lot
But not as much as here
I do believe this is a spot
Where raindrops fall all year

But on the plus side in the Bont
When sun shines it is bright
And I can sunbathe if I want
Or moon bathe through the night

It is very quiet in Pontarddulais
Not loud and noisy like the town
I think I'll stay in Pontarddulais
And I won't move around.

James Lockwood (12)
Pontarddulais Comprehensive School

DRAGON CAT

Yellow eyes aglow
Like city neon lights
Yellow eyes are like
The spotlight of
The farmyard nights.

He is behind you
He'll always find you
Fiery breathing
Hissing and steaming
His dragon heart fiery
He's crafty and wiry.

A face to turn milk sour
Beak-like grin and claws
Large and pointed ears
Teeth dagger sharp
To pierce and inspire fears.

His demon pointed tail
And his caterwauling wail
The creeping, glaring sparkling features
A truly awe-inspiring creature.

Alex Whitehead (12)
Pontarddulais Comprehensive School

The Roller Hockey Match

I take off my trainers,
I put on my blades,
I see my reflection in the barricades.
I step out onto the arena,
Are we gonna win? I must be a dreamer.
I put on my gloves, I pick up my stick,
I put on my helmet, God I feel sick!
We're in the cup final, hip hip hooray,
The ref blows his whistle, come on let's play.
We steal the ball and make an attack,
I pass it to Wayne, who passes to Jack,
Jack takes a shot, it's wide of the post,
I thought he had scored it had gone so close.
I chased the ball, as fast as I could,
as it touched my stick I knew that I should,
I swung back my stick to an incredible height,
Then saw the ball burst into flight.
Higher and higher the ball seemed to get,
Then dipped down low and into the net.
We were winning one-nil, ahead of the rest,
The crowd kept on shouting . . .
The Pythons are best!

James Rogers (12)
Pontarddulais Comprehensive School

LEE BRENNAN

Lee Brennan that was his name
I really fancied him not because of his fame
I thought he was lovely and it was a crime
For anyone else to like him, I thought he was mine.

I wanted to meet him to tell him I cared
But he might just laugh, I'd be really scared
How do you tell someone you don't know
What you feel for them just won't go?

There was a competition on the radio
To meet 911, I really wanted to go
That competition I lost, I was so sad
Another girl won it, I thought she was bad.

I was unhappy all that night
I just laid on my bed, and turned off the light
In the darkness I felt so low
I really loved him, but I couldn't let him know.

I knew in my heart if I'd get the chance
No longer alone to his songs I would dance
But I was just kidding myself all the time
I'm just a fan, his heart will never be mine.

Carys James (12)
Pontarddulais Comprehensive School

FOOTBALL

Everybody singing and I hear the crowd roar,
They start kick off a goal everyone wants more,
Manchester U 1 Liverpool 0,
I am in the crowd I cannot sit still
Penalty, Giggs comes to take it
Come on he has to make it,
He is drowning in sweat, here he goes,
It is in the back of the net,
After half time the score is the same,
Wow this is a good game,
The score is still 2-0,
And this game is brill.
'Ole ole ole' we hear, the crowd sing,
Cole fell down I think he has pulled a limb,
The whistle has to go,
Liverpool supporters shout 'No!'
The final score was 2-0,
God that game was brill,
I want a hot dog from the store,
But the man says that there are no more.

Jack Joseph (12)
Pontarddulais Comprehensive School

SEA AND LAND

Fish are bright
Fish are tight
Fish like food straight from the flows
Fish eat worms that are treats
Fish swim like the wind
Fish look at their prey
Fish I eat
Fish I keep.

I love pets
I hate debts
I love frogs
I love dogs.

Food is lovely, especially sweeties
Food is nice, I love rice
Food, I eat food, I sleep
Food is lovely, I eat curry.

Sport is brilliant
Sport is cool
I love sport with my toys
Sport is cool at school.

Lino Davies (11)
Pontarddulais Comprehensive School

MAGNUS POWERMOUSE

Magnus was a big mouse,
He was as big as a house.
He ate all day,
Especially the month of May.

He is bigger than his mother,
Nothing like his father.
He isn't frightened of cats,
He even chases bats.

All his brothers are dead
Because he squashed their heads.
He's an only child,
He likes his cheese mild.

Magnus was called the powermouse,
Because he was there to save his house.
He hugs his mother and squishes her,
And calls his father Sir.

Marcus and Madeleine love their baby boy,
To make him quiet they give him a toy.
He is such a big mouse,
Now he can't fit in his house.

Leanne Lloyd (13)
Pontarddulais Comprehensive School

FRIENDS

Friends are good,
Friends are cool,
Friends are fun,
Friends are there for everyone.

Some are tall,
Some are short,
Some are in-between,
Some are nice and clean.

Friends are tidy,
Friends are messy,
Friends are a bit of both,
Friends take you out on a boat.

Some are happy,
Some are sad,
Some are in the middle,
Some have to fiddle.

Friends are good,
Friends are cool,
Friends are fun,
Friends are there for everyone.

David Gower (12)
Pontarddulais Comprehensive School

THE FOUR SEASONS

Spring, summer, autumn, winter,
Are the four seasons of the year.
The smell of spring just wakes me up,
The seeds are scattered for sowing.

Summer is the best season,
We get cherry red,
Then turn brown,
We go on holiday to have a break.

Autumn is joyful,
Red, brown, yellow and orange leaves.
Are the joyful colours,
Leaves go crusty,
When you touch it, it will crumble.

Winter is fun,
Even though we see little sun.
It is cold and shivery in the night,
It goes dark early and can give you a fright.
But Christmas comes early in winter,
When we celebrate Jesus Christ's birthday.
We give presents and except presents from friends
And family, which warms us all with happiness and joy.

Kali-Ann Joseph (11)
Pontarddulais Comprehensive School

BRAINY FLEAS

My dog died of fleas
When they bit into his brain,
I didn't know what happened
When he suddenly went insane.
He tried to bite his nose off
But he didn't quite succeed.
He bit half his tail off
Then tried to bite his lead.
He died a slow death in his bed
As the fleas came jumping out
Barking and fetching sticks.
How did I figure it out!

We buried my pet dog
In a cardboard box.
Then out jumped the fleas
Onto a passing fox.
I didn't really care
As it wasn't my own pet.
What really upset me
Was I saw it with a vet.
Someone must stop them
From biting into brains
Because I really do think
I'll go insane.

Rachel Buckley (12)
Pontarddulais Comprehensive School

The Football Game

Today we have a football game
Oh what a match it will be,
With the audience laughing out loud
as soon as they set eyes on me.

I get out on the pitch
and kick the ball,
I try four goals
and miss them all.

Michael's laces already undone,
Martin's shorts are not pulled up,
We'll never win that
Golden cup.

Ten minutes left then . . .
Hip hip hooray,
Jason scores
and saves the day.

Five minutes left,
Oh what a shame.
We need one more goal
to win the game.

I can't believe it!
Joseph scored,
we won the game
our coach was called.

He gave us the cup
and said to the crowd,
'To be their coach,
I'm very proud.'

Sarah Probert (11)
Pontarddulais Comprehensive School

My Brother

My brother is a pain,
Richard is his name,
He drives me insane,
And I always get the blame.

He hogs the telly,
And always stuffs his belly,
The sight of him isn't very merry
He looks like a bowl of green jelly.

He says that I'm fat
And that one day I'm going to kill the cat
But it's him who's fat
And smells like a dead rat.

Him and his designer gear,
And he thinks he is cool drinking his beer,
But cool he is nowhere near,
And without his mummy he is full of fear.

We don't get along very well
I suppose by now you can tell
When he's nice he lets me borrow his gel
And he once helped me up when I fell.

Rhian Horlock (14)
Ysgol Gyfun Gwyr

ENEMIES IN KOSOVO

Enemies locked in battle,
Innocent people die.
It's a war that no one can settle,
Relatives with lasses cry.

Bombs rain down from the sky,
Homes are demolished fast,
People flee to mountains high
Afraid to let go of their past.

The cold of winter is coming,
Makeshift homes are built,
Clothes and food are lacking,
Yet no one accepts guilt.

Owain Gimblett (14)
Ysgol Gyfun Gwyr

THE FAIRY

She jumps into the thin blue air
With dainty toes and long blonde hair
A little face with clothes so bare
She's a fairy, no need to stare

Her see-through wings like shiny crystals
So fragile you can see it glisten
Her skin so white, white as clouds
Her ears so sensitive, not too loud

A magical scene is seeing a fairy
It's not often you see one . . .
Very rarely.

Zöe Rasmussen (14)
Ysgol Gyfun Gwyr

ESCAPE

As I gaze through the glass,
The sun burns black,
Twisted metal holds me in,
Beads of cold sweat glisten,
On my shaking skin,
The sharp suffering pleasure,
I'm sinking into bliss,
I lick my lips to receive your kiss,
You fill my veins with burning chill,
Without you I fade,
This room my cell,
These walls my mirrors,
My world is here,
There's no escape.

Angharad Jones (14)
Ysgol Gyfun Gwyr

PAIN

A world of terror,
people panicking,
doubtful children being moved from country to country.
Men fighting for their lives,
two countries playing a game of wrestling.

A world as black as fog swallowing night.
Harmless people starving, suffering,
empty tubes of buildings on fire, being destroyed like a bonfire.
God disappeared,
and Hitler came.

Gemma Waters (14)
Ysgol Gyfun Gwyr

DIFFERENT WORLD

I walked around the corner
There was a light,
Then a flash,
Then a flicker.

Everything had gone,
It was just a field
People were wearing weird things
Shorts on their heads
T-shirts on their feet.

They said things backwards
The sea was pink
The grass was white.
There were fish flying in the air.

It was all wrong
I realised I was in Mirrorland
'A different world' completely.

Lara Bragger (14)
Ysgol Gyfun Gwyr

THE WINDOW

As I look out of the window,
It opens a whole new book of colours,
In the summer all bright colours,
And in the winter all dull colours.

Every summer when I draw the curtains,
I look out at the colours of summer,
The blue sky, the green grass and an array of flowers,
And the birds and butterflies fluttering their wings.

In the winter I see a different scene,
I look out at the white canvas, that covers the land,
Children building snowmen and throwing snowballs,
Winter is surely my favourite scene.

It doesn't matter which season it is,
I love looking out of my window,
I look out when I wake up and before I go to bed,
It brightens me up every day.

Ffion Davies (14)
Ysgol Gyfun Gwyr

HELP!

Writing a poem,
what a terrible task.
The family run
whenever I ask.

But, no help for me
alone must I struggle.
Writing this poem,
my mind is a muddle.

At my desk I sit,
trying for a rhyme.
But all that I pass
is a long, long time.

Iambic pentameters,
what a joke!
This is no occupation
for a good looking bloke.

Ian Davies (14)
Ysgol Gyfun Gwyr

ALONE

As I sit here looking,
My thoughts are far away,
Thinking of the good times,
Blotting out memories of that day.

You left me full of promises,
On that glorious September morn,
Duty was to your country,
I waited up for news until dawn.

The news came through suddenly,
A loss of my innocent man,
Here I am reminiscing,
Alone - 'my hero' - my special Dan.

Laura Beveridge (14)
Ysgol Gyfun Gwyr

A DIFFERENT WORLD

I bet this world would make you think,
you will be there in just a wink.
Wishing wells and magic lamps,
comedy galore and funny pranks.
Trees filled with money and sweets too,
Disney characters like Winnie the Pooh.
There's other things like moving floors,
I'd watch out here there's killer doors.
Have you ever seen a purple cat?
There are plenty here I can tell you that!
I think we had better leave right now,
I thought I saw a flying cow.

James Owen (15)
Ysgol Gyfun Gwyr

THE FUGITIVE

On the run,
Nowhere to go,
He hides in doorways,
To and fro.

The wind brushing
through his hair,
As he stands in fright,
Full of despair.

Not even his shadow can he trust,
Friend or foe,
No one he can turn to,
Full of woe.

Angharad Roberts (13)
Ysgol Gyfun Gwyr

DEAD END

Today, tomorrow and a tear for yesterday,
Death, murder and massacre,
A dead dove on the roadside and
A dead peace keeper in his untimely grave,
Godly hands stained with guilty blood,
Misty recollections of the beloved,
Hypocritical religion and holy books that weep,
Cold figures of stone-cold bodies,
Vacant signs hang on Heaven's door,
No questions asked and no answers given,
No way out and no way back,
Dead end.

Nia M Seaton (16)
Ysgol Gyfun Gwyr

CONTINUUM

Lost in the vast ocean of nothing -
A nothing which is my life.
A small ship is tossed across the waves -
A ship which is my hope.
Black waves engulf the ship with white claws -
Waves which are my fears.
A sharp gust of wind tips the ship once more -
The wind which is my sorrowful sigh.
The rain pounds down upon the ship -
Raindrops which are my tears.
The stars wink cruelly from the sky -
Stars which are my enemies.
The sky, a canvas, empty and black -
An emptiness which fills my heart.
The luminous moon, steadily glowing -
A glow which is my soul.
Dark clouds suffocate the moon -
Clouds which are society.
The steady moon, trapped by space -
A trap which is the system.
The system chokes the ones who dare -
The one who is myself.
My ship fights a valiant battle -
A battle to be itself.
Its weapons bombard the fearsome waves -
The weapon is my identity.
The battle, for once, a humanitarian cause -
The cause, to preserve mankind.

Gwenllian Thomas (16)
Ysgol Gyfun Gwyr

MORTALITY VERSUS IMMORTALITY

Tick, tock, tick, tock.

Imagine that time did not exist,
had no meaning, and we all lived forever. Imagine.

The Earth,
tethered by an invisible force to a burning sphere,
would, (give or take a few million) become grossly overpopulated.
And our own immortality would force us to live,
crammed, crushed, choked, desperate.

We could not starve,
for we live forever.
Although we still feel the hunger.
Asphyxiation, disease, thirst, could never kill us.
A world of immortals
controlled.
We must suffer the pain.
The ugly, hateful truth that immortality is not as much fun
as God made it out to be. Imagine.

But we are mortal. Visitors on a rock hurtling through time and space.
This we take for granted,
whilst refusing to believe that our actions lead to our destruction.
That deforestation has no more effect on us,
than a butterfly beating its wings halfway around the world.
Of course mortality enables love to last forever,
and one lifetime gives us enough of the universe to appreciate.
But carefully, carefully tread your way
for tick, an opportunity for good fortune disappears.
Tock, an opportunity for love, gone.
Tick, tock, tick, tock
until all is lost.

Kelly Griffiths (17)
Ysgol Gyfun Gwyr

FINALITY

For now
I have no fear of death.
Lusting for that endless feeling,
Yearning for a blank space to fulfil me.

My anger gone
My death.

Seeping sorrows
Like a tide.
Sadness overwhelming.

The final conclusion.

The only way out from my casting shadows.
The last glimmer of hope,
Leaving
Pain and anger
Turned inward behind me.

The stillness of my body,
The life within -
Gone.
Casting shadows have ceased . . .

This is the death within me
No longer waiting to be expressed.

Lisa Marie De Benedictis (15)
Ysgol Gyfun Gwyr

My Friend

Wake up! It's morning sleepy head!
Pink tongued and yawning,
She stretches out of bed.

'Time to play' bright eyes expecting,
Ears up high,
Ready to go 'fetching'!

Out into the garden, prancing,
Leaping to the bouncing ball,
Proudly fetching and returning,
Crouches, waiting my next call.

Smiley-faced with blown-back ears,
She bounds across the windswept sands,
Gulls rise, screeching, fleeing wildly,
Back she runs at my command.

But poor postman, milkman, neighbour,
You're intruders on her land,
Head back, barking, growling, threatening,
Powerfully she makes her stand.

She's my minder, she's my hero,
She defends me to the end,
Sometimes nasty, sometimes nutty,
She's the world's best ever friend!

Ffion Davies (11)
Ysgol Gyfun Gwyr

LET'S PARTY

Four girls together,
all in a tether.
We're all getting excited,
as we've all been invited.

A disco party,
for Richard Hearty.
He's the birthday boy host,
and he's better looking than most.

What should we do with our hair?
What should we wear?
Hot pants or peddlers,
boob tube or hipsters.

We all help each other,
with eye shadow and blusher.
We all fight for the mirror,
as the time draws nearer.

We arrive at the gate,
at a quarter past eight.
We enter half hearted,
as the party's all ready started.

The lights are all flashing,
which makes the boys dashing.
The music's real loud,
but it goes with the crowd.

We all dance together on the dance floor,
when the music stops we all shout for more.
We dance the whole night with barely a stop,
by the end of the evening we were ready to drop.

Although this time no luck with a date.
Who gives a monkey's, the party was great.

Rhiannon Pace (15)
Ysgol Gyfun Gwyr

A Different World

Do we realise, in our cosy environment,
How other people live in this world of ours?
Do we appreciate when we go to bed at night
Our warm duvet and the peace of hours,
Of sleep undisturbed.
No crying of siblings, no worry of soldiers,
They rely on the generosity of people like us,
Taking up their cry for help.
But how many hear that plea for equality?
How many respond to the pitiful state
Of those we see on the television
Our way of life would be luxury to them
The things in life that we take for granted.
If only the countries could forget
Their differences
And work together to ensure fair play
What a different world for everyone to live in
Our planet at peace and benefiting all.

Ceri-Llian James (15)
Ysgol Gyfun Gwyr

Out Of This World

Metallic floors,
Automatic doors,
Push button controls,
On silver panelled walls.

Sounding alarms,
Buzzers, ringing bells,
Calling attention,
To give information.

Oval shaped windows,
Where I view galaxies,
Bright stars and new worlds,
There is much more to see.

Curon Wyn (13)
Ysgol Gyfun Gwyr

Fireworks

Whoosh, bang there another one goes,
Ooh, aah, the crowds are on their toes.
Crimson, indigo, gold and green,
There's a rocket, what a scream.

Twirling, swirling and bouncing,
That one looks like it's dancing.
Lots of babies crying,
The fireworks are dying.

And everyone will always remember,
The 5th of November.

Carys Jenkins (12)
Ysgol Gyfun Gwyr

Slow Motion

I wonder what the world would be like in slow motion,
People going about their business at half the speed,
No one rushing or running,
Birds gracefully hovering in the sky,
Their prey crawling and scuttling slowly on the ground.

The earth revolving around the sun sluggishly,
A day lasting 48 hours instead of 24,
The whole world seems motionless,
No racing clouds,
Just a blanket of white foam sweeping across the land,
No fast-running waves crashing on the sand,
Only their faint echoes to be heard.

Hardly any sound anywhere,
Only people's mumbles as they try to string together a sentence,
Talking is meaningless,
Life is pointless in a world so slow.

Bethan Edwards (14)
Ysgol Gyfun Gwyr

Beach

The empty beach,
Grey sand covers,
The footprints of
Long lost lovers.
There is no fun
The beach is empty,
Winter has come.

Elizabeth Jones (15)
Ysgol Gyfun Gwyr

A Magical Scene

I kicked my feet through crumpled leaves,
Of yellow, red and brown,
And through the trees so very bare,
A golden sun shone down.

It glistened over everything,
With a beautiful, magical glow,
And the birds up high were singing,
So that everyone would know.

And I saw the happy faces,
Of the people on my way,
And I thanked the Lord for giving us,
A perfect autumn day.

Bethan Way (15)
Ysgol Gyfun Gwyr

Darkness

It's dark and quiet,
The air is tense,
My heart echoes around the room,
Like a thousand beating African drums,
I lie there quiet and still,
Daring not to move at all for fear of disturbing the quietness.
What's that noise? Creaking, squeaking,
Then suddenly there's a knock,
A loud, loud knock,
Then comes the noise I've been dreading,
'Come on love, it's time to get up!'
Then I know I'm doomed
It's a school day.

Natalie Saunders (14)
Ysgol Gyfun Gwyr

THE BOOK

The book I found was dusty,
The cover on it was musty,
It was locked up in the attic,
And no one had ever unpacked it,
So now it had gone all crusty.

Because the people who made it weren't trusty,
And neither were they fussy,
The pages were smudged,
And they'd never been budged,
So now the clasp and hinges were rusty.

The pictures in it were funny,
One was of a bunny,
He was sitting on a chair,
Talking to a hare,
And eating a pot of honey!

Christian Densley (15)
Ysgol Gyfun Gwyr

THE NIGHT SKY

I look and see a moonlit sky,
with stars which shine so brightly.
The midnight air is cold and crisp,
and the darkness stares around me.

Trees sway back and forth,
with a light breeze blowing their branches,
the waves crash, hitting rocks beneath me.
The stars like crystals in a dark black sky.

This is a dark winter's night.

Elinor L Jenkins (14)
Ysgol Gyfun Gwyr

A Magical Scene

The stars above were softly gleaming,
And frost was on the village roofs,
The bonfire was brightly burning,
Under the silvery moon.

The flames were spitting, swirling, flying,
And logs were cracking, roaring, glowing,
The smoke was twirling, creeping, choking,
Under the silvery moon.

The rockets hissed high into the sky,
And Catherine wheels swirled brightly,
Pleasant, happy faces gathered round,
Under the silvery moon.

Gorgeous, precious, gleaming jewels,
Soaring flames danced in the night,
Sparklers held by eager children,
Under the silvery moon.

The red hot flames begin to die,
The embers were lying by,
Ashes formed along the ground,
Under the silvery moon.

Catrin Morgan (14)
Ysgol Gyfun Gwyr

Polar Bear

A big white teddy bear rolling in the snow.
An endangered species under threat from human scum,
It only lives its life, like we live ours.
An elegant animal with its snow-white fur blowing in the wind.
Barely visible in the snow except a slight difference in shade.

Bang! A gun shot, red on white,
A stream of blood runs down the snow,
A white carcass lies still in a cold breeze.
Unfortunately they will die out,
They will be missed.

Rhys Padarn (14)
Ysgol Gyfun Gwyr

HOMELESSNESS

Days, months, years go by,
The years fly for many . . . the wealthy ones,
But the hours and days drag for me,
As I crouch shamefully on the corner of streets
Begging for money just to survive.
In the cold winters,
I sit shivering in my tatty old rags,
They lack the warmth I long to feel,
Staring at strangers strutting past confidently in their
                                    warm cosy clothes.
I listen as they moan to each other about their 'so-called'
                                    worries and problems . . .
They don't even know they're born!
Their lives are my fantasies, my dream is to be 'normal'.
I am looked down on like dirt . . . I might as well not be here!
I do not crave material things,
I merely long to be able to look forward to returning home,
                                    to a loving family . . .
But have no one, except for my dog, my trusty companion,
To whom I would give my last . . . he is all I have to love.
Some would say I am lucky to be alive, they are naive!
- What they don't realise is . . .
I am alive but alone!

Andráea Parker (14)
Ysgol Gyfun Gwyr

A Hallowe'en Party

Ghosts, witches and Dracula,
going trick or treating tonight,
if you open the door
you might just get a fright.

Loud, gothic music playing at the party down the street,
Phantom of the Opera, Dracula or ghosts
just who will you meet
as you party on down to the beat?

Scary costumes, everywhere and anywhere
going to the party.
I don't recognise those people under there,
so what! Why don't I join them for a dare.

Twelve o'clock,
it's the middle of the night,
come, come to the haunted party down the street,
and I can assure you'll have a big, *big fright!*

Christopher Huw Davies (14)
Ysgol Gyfun Gwyr

Winter

The leaves are falling
It's very cold
The wind is blowing
It's very cold.
The sun has gone
The rain is here.
No more people.
Winter is here.

Rhys Jones (14)
Ysgol Gyfun Gwyr

THE FOREST

As I walk down the path,
The mud caked, twig strewn path,
The forest beckons,
Drawing me in with it's leafy peace,
It's shadowy shelter
And its tapestry silence.
I enter and time stands still.
Long creaking arms reach out to embrace me.
Enfolding me in their knobbled prison.
The light dims,
Bright sunshine replaced by fingers of lemon light
Dappling the earth floor with honey.
Above my head, huge majestic trees stretch upwards,
Straining to touch the criss-cross mosaic of blue sky.
Sheltering beneath the bulk of a gnarled old oak
A duster of bluebells nod a greeting in the breeze.
Quiet covers everything like a thick blanket.
All about me moss shrouded trees
Seem to stand to attention like soldiers,
Silently waiting . . . waiting . . . eternally waiting.
Now I must leave the forest with it's leafy peace.
Shadowy shelter and tapestry silence.
For it is not here that I belong.
My place is back in the noisy, bustling,
Never silent world.
Yet soon I shall return to the forest,
My only oasis of peace in a world of noise,
My only sanity in a world of madness.

Alice Loft (14)
Ysgol Gyfun Gwyr

Why Do People?

Why do people argue?
And to what good does it come?
And why do people laugh?
Just to spite someone?

Why do people hunt?
Stealthily they kill,
Ignoring all the protests,
And seeing faces fill,
With anger, with hate, with disbelief,
At the horrific acts fulfilled.

Savagely they walk,
Possessed by cold-bloodied minds,
So selfishly and so robotically,
Ignoring all the signs.

Not one ounce of love
In their mindlessly beating hearts,
To kill is a reckless sin
But still,
Wickedly they laugh.

Sara Moran (14)
Ysgol Gyfun Gwyr

December Nights

Clear and icy pincushioned sky,
Cold white frost bitter on your cheeks
Smoky breath and tingly toes,
Long December nights bring sharpness to my world.

Voices echo in the icy air,
Footsteps crack on steel hard floors,
December nights how crisp and cold
A winter world of magic.

Warm glowing light shines,
Through windows.
Like pagan fathers
We are drawn to fire
To burn, to warm, to melt.

Friendly fire burn bright
As the steely stars reel round,
And stretch forever.
December nights so cold and still.
Even as the earth is spinning.

Lisa M Evans (14)
Ysgol Gyfun Gwyr

GOOD RIDDANCE

Another turning point,
A fork stuck in the road,
Time grabs you by the wrist
Directs you where to go
It's not a question,
But a lesson learned in time.

It's something unpredictable,
But in the end is right
I hope you had the time of your life.

So take the photographs,
And still frames in your mind,
Hang it on a shelf in good health,
And good time.

It's something unpredictable,
But in the end is right,
I hope you had the time of your life.

Amy Williams (15)
Ysgol Gyfun Gwyr

FIRE FLIGHT

First she's here
And then she's not
Where's she gone
I know not!

There she stands
So strong and bright
Showing off to all in sight!

Her name is *Fire Flight!*
Her coat as black as night
Her face a pretty sight.

Her mane as black as the ace of spades
A never ending stream
Gleaming in all its might.

There she goes so bold and bright
Like a streak of lightning in the night
Round the corner - off she goes
As she gallops out of sight . . .

Rhian John (14)
Ysgol Gyfun Gwyr

WHY IS THERE WAR?

Here I am tucked up in bed
And absolutely no worries ahead.
Across the globe and down the road
A war is breaking out . . .

Maybe it's because two families feud
Maybe it's because the neighbours are rude.
Maybe it's because of the country's wealth
Think of all the children there - all by themselves.

Maybe one day I'll be in a war.
To hear all the guns and engines roar,
People shouting children crying
I don't understand the war.

Rebekah Smitham (13)
Ysgol Gyfun Gwyr

HITLER'S GERMANY

Footsteps sinking into the darkness,
Voices echoing through the night,
Necks are turning and are staring
Looking at the world with fright.

Bombs are landing and exploding,
Shattering poor helpless lives,
Dead corpses lie around the streets,
Swarming round like yellow beehives.

Hands are raising slowly,
To the pale man with a moustache,
He's talking a load of promises,
That ears are pleased to hear.

'He's promised to give us things,
That we couldn't normally afford,
He is brilliant, he's the best,
We will surely vote for him.'

The quiet voices chant 'Hail Hitler'
Like silent whispers in the wind,
And lonely tears fall down,
The face of a nation.

Rhianwen Davies (14)
Ysgol Gyfun Gwyr

DEATH BY DRUGS

Damp isolation
Small walls closing in.
Outside world - a stranger
Inside world - a fear!

Depressing danger
Stoned faces surround me.
One inhalation to happiness
One sniff further to death.

One sniff further to death,
One inhalation to happiness.
Stoned faces surround me
Depressing danger.

Inside world - a fear
Outside world - a stranger
Small walls closing in
Damp isolation

Death by drugs . . .

Verity Jones (14)
Ysgol Gyfun Gwyr

EVACUATION . . .

I saw my mother waving in the distance.
You wonder if you will ever see her again.
I remember she told me through her smiles and tears
And gave me the wish, through years grown strong.

The gentle spitting rain against my face
The emptiness you feel inside.
The fear is just too hard to hide
My mother is gone, but for how long?

The bombs hit the ground like droplets of water
I hide for shelter underground.
The noises are like earthquakes, thundering to me
That's my life . . . as an evacuee!

Rachel Anderson (13)
Ysgol Gyfun Gwyr

ALONE

Alone the stone stretches in the morning sun.
An island of strength it guards the centuries,
And saluting proud and straight
It greets each day.

Tall and square against the sky it stands,
Not a delicate beauty like the butterfly
That visits for a moment,
Before it drifts away on waves of time.

But out of the mists of history
It transcends this life,
Solid in its solitary sojourn
On this lonely earth.

Steadily, the stone watches over the land,
Unmoved by the moaning wind,
Unflinching in the sun's dragon-breath,
Unchanged by rain and hail.

Alone in the moonlight, memories
Of an ancient race worshipping the sky,
Visit its dreams.

Trystan Rice (14)
Ysgol Gyfun Gwyr

ALONE

I'm surrounded by everything -
yet I'm all alone.

Crashing notes of the great
Symphonies thunder all
Around, jostling,
Fighting for a space to
Ignite into
Glorious flames of passion and beauty.

Crystal raindrops plummet from a
Sapphire sky; Fire-bright
Rainbows shatter in a silent
Explosion of colour and light, then
Fly off as dazzling fireflies
To light a saddened heart.

I can hear the silence
Ruffling the air with long
Ghostly fingers - fingers that
Pinch, tweak fear, sadness and
Loneliness from hearts of stone,
Cradle greed.

The darkness blinds and
Dazzles, suffocating and
Choking. Shadows creep and
Send ice-hot shivers through my
Spine, burning and melting
Happiness to oozing tar -

I'm all alone.

Sarrah Morgan (16)
Ysgol Gyfun Gwyr

LOVE

Cupid with his golden arrow,
Shooting all, wide and narrow,
Never hitting the right pair,
Like missing targets at a fair.

Hit one here,
Miss one there,
Lovesick people everywhere.

Get some arrows to reverse,
All the down-sides of this verse,
Like miss matches all around,
Love for them cannot be found.

Cupid leave love up to fate,
Or learn to shoot your arrows straight,
In love I find myself entwined,
But yet true love, I never find.

Holly Davies (15)
Ysgol Gyfun Gwyr

MAGICAL SCENE

I dreamed I saw you
Standing in a Pacific sunset.
Watching the wild waves
Pounding the jagged rocks.
The whistling wind ruffling your hair.
Your cheeks as pink as peaches.
The cool breeze on your pure, soft face.
Your hand holding mine
Would be a perfect dream . . .

Cari Griffiths (12)
Ysgol Gyfun Gwyr

ALONE!

I am alone like an ugly scarecrow
Sad, I bow my head down low.
Beneath the wind and rain
Winter gales and snow.
I am alone like the cold wind
Full of birds' cries,
restless as a shorn sheep
bitter with weary eyes.

I am alone like a babbling brook.
Not knowing where I'm heading
as harmless as a worm,
struggling, slipping, sliding.
I am alone like a winter robin,
quivering against the wind that drives,
hopping and swerving
glancing with rapid eyes.

I am alone like a wild cat,
fighting to survive.
Creeping, waiting, as silent as the grave.
Crouching, listening and hoping.
I am alone like a tree in winter,
reaching out for company, praying,
dreaming of warmer days.
Cold and bare, anxious - longing . . .

Rhian Ivey (14)
Ysgol Gyfun Gwyr

THE SWEET SHOP

Fudge and toffee piled up high,
Orange lollipops as tall as the sky.
Fruity jelly beans in great big jars
Chocolates hiding in plastic cars.

White mice and strawberry laces
Sherbet fountains and jelly faces.
Strips of round boiled sweets
And other tasty, colourful treats.

To a child, this place is like a dream,
Full of chocolate, sugar and cream.
The mouth-watering odour
Makes you want to come back for more . . .

Rhiannon Morgan (14)
Ysgol Gyfun Gwyr

THE 5TH OF NOVEMBER!

The spark of light,
Blue, green and white.
The whooshing and screeching
Of bonfire night . . .

An unforgettable time.
The sky filled with colours.
The colours of jewels,
Silver, gold and lime . . .

The 5th of November
Oh! How I remember . . . !

Rhian Nurse (12)
Ysgol Gyfun Gwyr

A Different World!

Wouldn't it be great
If there was a place
Where everywhere - was a famous face!
They're yellow men from Timbuktu
With little Piglet and Winnie the Pooh.
There's Mickey, there's Minnie
And Pluto the dog.
There's even a prince who turned into a frog!
I tell you all this because it is true
This place is meant for me and you.
Lay down your head and you will see
There's much, much more than HTV!
Close your eyes and enjoy the ride
Push all bad thoughts to one side.
Of all the things that you have seen
This is beyond your wildest dream.
You are here with me - we will have such fun
After all this dream - has only just begun . . .

Bethan Reddy (13)
Ysgol Gyfun Gwyr

The War

Running, hiding, shooting, fighting
bombing, screaming, ducking, diving.
Rampaging, raging, thrashing, smashing
Will this war ever end?

Scream over here
Scream over there
If only I had another hand to spare
Will this war ever end?

When the war started, we were a team
The war is ending and I feel alone
All is quiet . . .
I think the war is over!

Rhiannon Reddy (13)
Ysgol Gyfun Gwyr

THE SHEPHERD'S STORY

It was a cold night
Out watching our sheep.
An Angel came down
To tell the good news . . .

The news that was told,
A Saviour has come.
He lies in a bed
In a cattle shed . . .

So we left the field
Went to Bethlehem.
We saw a great star
Over a stable . . .

Inside the stable
Lay the Messiah
Our simple present
To him was a lamb . . .

Then back to our sheep
We went praising God
For his gift to us
Jesus our Saviour . . .

Iestyn Austin (14)
Ysgol Gyfun Gwyr

GHOSTLY SILENCE

A pale white ghostly figure standing
silently in the darkness
staring at me with its wide golden eyes.
Frightening thoughts entered my mind as
the whistling wind rushed through the trees.

The silent night air was damp
and I choked on a cloud of misty cold air.
My wet hair clung tightly to my warm body.

The see-through figure carefully stepped forward,
I stumbled away - sweating.
My heart was pounding rapidly, as a gust of wind
crept down my spine.

I looked and shuddered as the ghost vanished into
the shadows.

Mari Jones (12)
Ysgol Gyfun Gwyr

GHOSTS!

A ghost is a pale white figure
A ghost is an icy breeze
A ghost is a daunting monster
A ghost is an evil creature.

A ghost is a frightening phantom
A ghost is a gruesome ghoul
A ghost is a lonely cry
You can't see it . . . but you can try!

Carys Pope (12)
Ysgol Gyfun Gwyr

A Winter Scene

Air all around is still and cold.
The sky slumbers by slowly.
With its white cotton clouds,
A mantle of snow covers the land
Like a sprinkling of white icing.

As you walk the snow bound earth,
It crunches like dry leaves.
You hear the whisper of bitter wind
As it weaves its cold ways around you.

Icicles descend from the trees
Like witches' fingers
Ready to stab you at anytime.
Trees are bashfully bare,
With no colourful leaves to clothe them.

Frozen lakes lay glassy still
Like windows to another world.
The windswept crust
Sparkles like countless clear crystals.

When night falls
All is still and silent.
And the moon shivers brightly
Over the winter world.

Abigail Ede (14)
Ysgol Gyfun Gwyr

YESTERDAY, TODAY, TOMORROW

Yesterday, today, tomorrow
The cycle began
We don't seem to care
Death as the consequence - is sure to be the result!

In a world of war and worry
Is there no peace?
In a cage of conflict and cruelty
Is there no freedom?

Yesterday, today, tomorrow.
The cycle began
We don't seem to care
Death as the consequence - is sure to be the result!

Our earth's heart is as precious as the
Indispensable air we breath.
Do we wish to taste it, choke on it?
Rather than thrive - live on it!

Yesterday, today, tomorrow
The cycle began
We don't seem to care
Death as the consequence - is sure to be the result!

Greed and indifference
By nation to nation.
Leave some parched and starved
While others drown in surfeit.

Yesterday, today, tomorrow
The cycle proceeds,
We know the problems,
But,
Will we act to solve them!

Siân Eleri Jones (15)
Ysgol Gyfun Gwyr

LOOKING THROUGH YOUR EYES . . .

If I looked back at the
Book of my past
I think I'd say
It went quite fast!

I aimed quite high
As high as the sky
But sometimes wished
That I could fly!

The things I did
And the things I said
Seemed to result in
Making me red.

They used to laugh
And used to stare
But what made them
Want to be so unfair?

Friends gave me a nudge
Said 'Don't be so down!'
But why did I always
Feel like a clown!

But why did they laugh
And why did they stare?
I don't think they knew
They were being unfair!

It's too late now
'Cause I'm way up high
But I can see what
Made me cry!

Leigh Alexandra Woolford (14)
Ysgol Gyfun Gwyr

HEAVEN

All beautiful things surrounding me
like flowers and roses.
The big bright sea
everything I like
and dreamed for me.
Oh! I want to swim that sea.

Families and friends now unite
they talk and laugh.
Oh! What a long night.
They start to argue
shout and scream.
They settle down
and finish the scene.

Samantha Swain (13)
Ysgol Gyfun Gwyr

THE FUGITIVE

I needed to get away
so I legged it to Swansea Bay.
I did nick a car
but I didn't get very far!

The car ran out of fuel
right by Brynmill School.
The sirens were gaining
and it started raining.

This is no way to live
perhaps I won't be a fugitive . . .

Carys Rees (13)
Ysgol Gyfun Gwyr

A Poem

It was a magical day, a day to remember.
A giant lemon burning
like a single and magnificent candle
surrounded in a blanket of blueness.
Tiny white balls sleeping peacefully
and the wind blowing softly on the body of the balls.
The sun smiled happily at the children below,
dancing like old boxes in the wind.
Multicoloured flowers dreaming and growing
peacefully on the arms of the trees.

But then the lemon faded slowly,
by welcoming a giant of a stone to the sky.
The stars peeped out of the darkness and
stared down on the earth like cats eyes.
And the entire sky still
still like the sea after a brutal storm.
Oh yes! This was a magical night
a night to remember . . .

Sara Griffiths (14)
Ysgol Gyfun Gwyr

The Fugitive

Running and running,
hiding and wandering,
around and around.
Looking for a safe place to stay,
food to eat, water to drink
and something to prove that I'm innocent.
As time goes by - I will get my freedom!

Suzannah Smyth (13)
Ysgol Gyfun Gwyr

HALLOWE'EN

Children running through the streets
all dressed up like demons.
Hoping to collect some treats
down at Mr Freemans.

Tonight they'll have a party
with pumpkins burning bright.
Spooky, scary, funny tales
told on this special night.

Ghosts and witches swirl about
ducking apples, trick or treat.
Come and join the fun they shout
there's pumpkin pie to eat!

Midnight chimes began to beat
it was the best of frights.
Lots were sleeping on their feet
On October's last night!

Iwan Palmer (12)
Ysgol Gyfun Gwyr

THE FUGITIVE

*F*eared by faces, frightened inside
*U*ndergone all the stresses, devoid of pride
*G*utsy and greedy has courage, not sense
*I*diotic, could not be more intense
*T*ormented and tortured - easy to tease
*I*nside there's a person nobody sees
*V*agrance and violence is all that shows
*E*verything gone - as loneliness grows . . .

Kelly Hall (14)
Ysgol Gyfun Gwyr

BOWLING

Getting shoes - pain
Running to a lane.
Tapping in your name
Having a drink
Given crisps.
Throwing a ball - *thud!*
As the ball bounces
Down the lane.
Bang! A strike!
Again and again
Hurrah! I've won the game!
Given a meal
Because I won the game.
Nothing, no cheers!
I wake up
It was just a dream
Well! I might win soon . . .

Grace Morgan (12)
Ysgol Gyfun Gwyr

THE FUGITIVE

The flash of lightning hits the tree
and I'm free.
The rain is coming down
as I run as quickly as I can!
The wind is blowing bitterly
as if to dry my skin.
I am lost and alone
running from home.
My life will not be the same
as now I'm a runaway . . . !

Sarah Daniel (13)
Ysgol Gyfun Gwyr

Peace

To wake up one day,
and find the world in perfect condition.
A world without war, hunger and misfortune.
But a world with justice, friendliness and peace.

There would be life beyond fighting and loneliness.
There wouldn't be pollution.
everyone would be safe
no one would be ill.

There wouldn't be trouble
and people would care, for animals in danger
like the big brown bear.
The trees would be safe in their homes,
the lush green forests.

Yes! it would be perfect to wake up one day,
and find us all in a big perfect world . . .

Gwyneth Thomas (12)
Ysgol Gyfun Gwyr

A Magical Scene

A colourful sky
There goes the white plane - *high!*
With mist . . . *following.*

A blue sea shines
With a bright ship - *sailing*
Dolphins . . . *swimming.*

A hot beach lay - *warm*
Relaxing on cream sand
Now sun . . . *melting low!*

Sophie C Dark (12)
Ysgol Gyfun Gwyr

The Fugitive

He runs from place to place
Steals from shop to shop
But when he's done and had his fun
He runs to find a door
And through a quiet place to nap.

When he wakes, he wakes to
Find a lonely person deep inside
He leaves his name in ink
To show he was here once
And hunts for food and drink.

He eats and drinks, but doesn't think about
How he could get caught stealing and
Feeling free to rest anywhere he likes
The Fugitive . . .

Hannah Morgan (13)
Ysgol Gyfun Gwyr

World Cup '98

World Cup started on the 10th of June.
People excited and over the moon.
Brazil got away with a 2-1 win
While most people laughed and put on a grin.

The World Cup ended with Brazil v France
But half-way through the game
Brazil didn't have much chance!

As France held the Cup
The crowd cheered loud
And all French supporters felt ever so proud . . .

Megan Davies (11)
Ysgol Gyfun Gwyr

THE FUGITIVE

He runs from town to town
To find a place to hide,
He's run before but never learned
There's a price to pay for a hideaway!

He's scared, hungry and cold
And needs to eat,
He takes the chance to steal a meal,
He could get caught, but with some luck
He might just get a tasty treat.

He manages to find a warm place to rest,
Somewhere quiet, somewhere safe,
He keeps a look-out all the time
Just in case the cops pass by!

Amy Evans (13)
Ysgol Gyfun Gwyr

SIZZLING HOT!

It's amazing that things don't sizzle away
In the heat of the scorching sun.
Snakes slide slowly, slowly
On the surface of the Sahara sands.

Sandstorms slowly pick up in the wind
Sending sand everywhere,
Sand sweeps to every corner
Of the hot, dry desert.

Camels take me over the sinking sand
To a spring or oasis,
'Some water quickly, please!' I pray
'I feel like I'm going to die!'

Angharad Jenkins (12)
Ysgol Gyfun Gwyr

THE FUGITIVE

Fugitive running quick
Among the trees and the muddy slick
Flashing storm, lights up the night
Revealing then - your hidden fright
Fugitive quickly run
For you know you've done nothing wrong
And after all you've waited for this freedom for so long.

Another flash, another rumble
Lots of crashes and the fugitive tumbles
Before long he can't feel his legs
Just a permanent throbbing in his head
And as his arms begin to go weak all he wants then is to
sleep
And finally fugitive has found
A new kind of freedom
A freedom profound!

Sarah Aggus (13)
Ysgol Gyfun Gwyr

Evacuation!

I remember the days when I was young.
The world was at peace and I had so much fun.
Our home was a happy place with plenty of love,
Each night I'd thank God in the heavens above.
Then came the day when we lost our luck.
The world was at war and the bombers struck.
Night after night the skies were ablaze
With enemy planes that came out of the haze.
After a time my parents had to make
A terrible decision for my safety's sake.
I was sent to live in a far away place,
A country village that the planes could not trace.
My heart was aching and full of pain
I long to be with my family again.
Now to God each night I send
A prayer and a hope that this war will end . . .

Rachael Gregory (13)
Ysgol Gyfun Gwyr

My Bike

Wherever I go
I go there on my bike.
I ride it when I'm happy
I ride it when I'm sad.
Whatever the weather
Whatever the time
I'm on my bike . . .

I climb the hills
I cruise through the lanes.
I fly down the slopes
But sometimes I fall . . .

A bike is a friend
A bike is always the same.
A bike never lets you down
A bike is a very loyal companion.

Rhys ap Gwent
Ysgol Gyfun Gwyr

I'M AN EVACUEE!

Here I stand in Liverpool
in the middle of World War Two.
I'm going to get some foster parents
but I might not get through.

My father's fighting in the war
I wish he was here with me.
My mother's a First Aid nurse
and I'm an evacuee.

I know one day my parents
will eventually,
end this everlasting war,
and then come back for me.

But now I'm waiting in sorrow
for the day they'll come back for me.
But for now I'll live in Liverpool
because I'm an evacuee.

There is an ounce of hope
in the pit of my heart.
For this has kept me going
from the very start.

Tyla Williams (13)
Ysgol Gyfun Gwyr

THE FUGITIVE

He sat quivering on the pavement,
his blue eyes covered with tears, reminiscing about the past.
Eight years gone by.

Happy he was, until one day
when he went to a new school.
A fresh start.
A big school, a little boy.
He felt out of place!

The bus had left him
at the old, grey gates
for the start
of what would be an adventure,
a new experience.
Hundreds of teachers. Thousands of children
Was there room for one more?

He decided that extra pupil would not be him.
So he ran, and ran, yet nowhere to hide.
He ran until his legs could no longer move.
He had fled, like a fugitive from a life of terror.

He had run, scared as ever,
into the hall of his former school.
He took a look around him,
and bellowed *'I am back!'*

Alun Rhys Chivers (13)
Ysgol Gyfun Gwyr

Park Memories

The sun is sparkling
Children come to caper
On the swings or on the slide.
They're always here to play.

The slide is still.
The swings are impelling,
The screaming and laughing,
Eternally heard.

The birds are nesting in the tree,
The grass is as green as an emerald sea,
The sun is shining. Hooray! Hooray!
We'll go out to play. Today! Today!

The rain is suddenly falling,
The ducks are blissful and wet.
The children in shorts and T-shirt
Jumping in puddles, drenched!

People sheltering underneath,
Trees and bandstands,
Drips dancing down their faces,
Hair like wet stringy mops.

The grass is sodden and damp,
Umbrellas out in all colours,
Some red, some blue,
Some purple, some grey,
The rain shall stop one day . . .

Carys Humphreys (12)
Ysgol Gyfun Gwyr

MILLENNIUM

What does the millennium mean to you?
What does it mean to me?
Is it a time for reflection
Or a giant, global party?

When the champagne pops, the music stops,
And the clocks strike in a new era,
Will we all shake hands across different lands,
Can it bring peace and happiness nearer!

Will all the computers go crazy?
How will we all cope - now we're lazy?
When all their memories are permanently erased
Will we humans recall the golden days!

Are aliens planning to arrive uninvited?
They must be near - they're often sighted.
Would they want to be part of a human celebration,
Perhaps together forming the ultimate creation?

Just what will God think of all the commotion
Will he be angry or give us promotion?
I hope the millennium means less pollution,
Could it signify a new evolution?

5,4,3,2,1 - it's here! The Millennium's here!
After all those years of waiting, we shed a tear.
Everyone claps and gives a deafening cheer,
Millennium magic for you and me -
See you at the universal party . . . !

Rhys Cullen (12)
Ysgol Gyfun Gwyr

A Magical Scene

Crisp, white soft snow
Everything so still . . .
Until . . .
Pieces of cloud fall from heaven,
A white whirlwind of feathers
Riding ferocious winds.

Dancing daffodils and shimmering snowdrops,
Swaying in a gently breeze . . .
Until . . .
Short, sharp bursts of rain cascade,
Stinging the faces of flowers
Who grin and bear it!

Hot, lazy days,
On a paradise sunshine beach . . .
Until . . .
Lions with silver manes
Roar and devour the beach.
Washing it for when tomorrow comes.

Brown leaves drift towards the ground,
Sighing on a gentle breeze . . .
Until . . .
Wild, wet, winds,
Whip the leaves cruelly
From their resting places.

Each of this quartet
A completely magical scene . . .
Until . . .

Sara Elinor Tuckey (12)
Ysgol Gyfun Gwyr

EVACUATION

In 1939 the bombs
began to fall
in my home town
they flattened all
the walls.

My mum and dad were
so afraid that our house
would be next
they put us on the train
and tied labels around
our necks.

They told us that we would
be safe where we were going
to stay
we helped the people looking
after us to milk and
make the hay.

We loved the people very much
made lots of friends
and helped them
everyday
but missed our parents very
much and knew we
couldn't stay.

And in 1945 we were glad to
be alive
and later that year we went
back home . . .

Nerys Thomas (13)
Ysgol Gyfun Gwyr

MY WAR FRIEND

Darkness fell upon us
The day that war was declared.
Silence descended all around
But not a word was said.

Our minds were in turmoil
Wondering what was in store.
Would it be weeks, or months
And many such questions galore.

Each night we covered the windows
With heavy black-out blinds.
No lights in town nor country
But bright beams from big searchlights.

Many children came on the train,
We saw them lined up in the gym.
One boy, Bill, came to live next door
Mrs Dodds took great care of him.

Bill and I gaily played.
Throughout long summer evenings.
Warriors, best friends overnight
Never thinking of bad things.

Towards the end of the war
Mrs Dodds' son was killed.
Through her sadness and her grief
She still made time for Bill.

When the war was over
I knew Bill would go away
But we heard his family had died in a raid
So Mrs Dodds said my best friend could stay.

Robin Jones (13)
Ysgol Gyfun Gwyr

WALES

I come from a land called Wales
Mountainous, hilly and green,
and rivers, valleys and dales
with views that have to be seen.

With treasures under the ground
Miners strong and bold,
Black diamonds and gold to be found
And raised to the surface and sold.

A land full of furnace and steel
Where the sky is crimson and red,
Where masters make money and deal
Where fields and grass lie dead.

A land full of chapels and song
Where pulpits and preachers abound.
When people sing in their own tongue
And choirs sing all the year round.

A land full of castles and towers
With battlements made to last,
Where knights fought for the power
And wars shaped the past.

A land full of rivers and streams
Canals, ponds and lakes,
Water bubbles, splashes and screams
From source to mouth it breaks.

A land of rugby and sport
Fullback, hooker and flanker,
Where battles and games are fought
And props are built like tankers.

Wherever the world I should roam
Whatever the sights I should see,
It's always nice to come home
Wales is a part of me!

Hannah Barrow (13)
Ysgol Gyfun Ystalyfera

A PICNIC SURPRISE

Mr and Mrs Price went out one day
into the country - not far away.
They went in their car with a hamper of food
for a picnic, you did rightly conclude!

They tootled along in their Metro - three door!
singing old songs and stamping the floor.
Chugging up hills, at the pace of a snail,
with a long line of Hells Angels close on their tail.

They came to a field and decided to stop
for sandwiches, cakes and cool fizzy pop.
They carried the hamper to a nice cosy spot
the sky was blue and the sun quite hot.

They looked at the scenery while eating their grub
when out of the hamper there crawled a big bug.
It took to the air with very great speed
Mrs P looked up to determine its breed!

'It looks like we're in for a shower, I feel'
'Rubbish!' said Arthur 'there's no cloud, my dear!'
With a whoosh and a bang and a horrible splat
a tiled bathroom shower . . . laid him out flat!

Jonathan Davies (14)
Ysgol Gyfun Ystalyfera

LIFE

Life can be sad,
Life can be sweet,
Life can be untidy,
And sometimes neat.

Life can be hectic,
When rushing to places,
Or sometimes calm,
With time to tie your laces.

Life can be a song,
With joy and happiness,
Life can be a pain,
With thousands of practices.

Life can be passionate,
Wild and dramatic,
Life can be obsessive,
Like a chocolate fanatic.

Life can be scary,
With witches and ghosts,
Life can be scrumptious,
Like jam on toast.

But without life,
it would be boring,
With no people, characters
Chattering or snoring.

Without life,
Our world,
An empty page
Where the world will weep.

So what I'm saying, without a lie
Enjoy your life before you *die!*

Gwenllian Richards (12)
Ysgol Gyfun Ystalyfera

WINTER

Winter nights are cold and dark
No more calling of the lark
The trees begin to lose their leaves,
And on the ground Jack Frost breathes,
Squirrels are preparing for their sleep
Into their dreys they will creep.

As the rain runs down the mountain
It hits the ground like a fountain,
One big flood across the road
There they jump, all the toads,
Jumping here, jumping there
It is like one big fair.

All the animals are taken in the barn
And all is quiet on the farm,
You can hear it from afar,
As I look up I can see the stars,
Then they have gone with one big bright light,
I stand and stare with such a fright.

The sky is lit up as far as you can see,
We watch in fright, my brother and me.

Emma Morgan (11)
Ysgol Gyfun Ystalyfera

THE SILHOUETTE

It's there all the time,
Is it just in my mind?
He's there every night,
they say it's just me
but he's there to see.
Is it on my bedroom wall?
He stays there every night but,
he gives me a fright.
It is not me in my mind
he is there all night
but in the day it goes away,
Is it just my shadow and the moonlight?
I slept with my bedroom light on last night
but there was nothing in sight.
I now know it's in my imagination,
it's my shadow, it wasn't a boy there
and there was no need to panic.

Ceri Wyn Lodwig (11)
Ysgol Gyfun Ystalyfera

THE HUNTER

He stands in the lonely dark
Watching his food play up.
He stands on his own staring at his snack
Making sure his food cannot see his bright orange back
Running, growling, jumping into place
Behind big trees so it doesn't see his face
Listening quietly, ready to pounce
Out he jumps, with a tremendous bounce
Within seconds it's all taking place,
The lion retires with blood on his face.

Leighton Howells (11)
Ysgol Gyfun Ystalyfera

NIGHT

Strange things happen at night
Which always gives me a fright
Like ghosts from the graveyard
And rock monsters which are hard
Or aliens form the sky
With massive spacecraft that fly
Which make me very scared
To go to my lovely bed.
I curl up nicely and sleep
Until the morning shall peep
But I see the old ghost
Nicking everybody's toast
But it's only my dog
Who's hungry as a fat hog.

Richard Brett Oliver Mallinson (13)
Ysgol Gyfun Ystalyfera

WHAT IF?

Tonight as I lay thinking here,
What if some wally climbed inside my ear.
I tossed and tumbled all night long,
and sang a silly song.
What if the bed bugs bite?
What if I start a fight?
What if my tarantula escapes?
What if my leg breaks?
What if I fall from a height?
What if the school catches fire?
What if I learn to leap?
      I can't get to sleep.

Caroline Louise Ashill (12)
Ysgol Gyfun Ystalyfera

The Moon

Some think it's made of chocolate,
Or maybe even cheese,
But personally I believe that it
is made of peas.

Look closely at the moon at night,
and what you think are craters,
are really bowls of vanilla ice,
surrounded by fat wafers.

I'd love to be an astronaut,
and rocket to the moon,
but if I went I'd take with me
a meteorite spoon.

Clementine Hollister (13)
Ysgol Gyfun Ystalyfera

The Firework Display

Multicoloured sparks,
in the deep dark sky;
Flames of the bonfire,
going way up high.
I watch them *pop,*
as they open up wide,
and let out the glitter
that's trapped inside.
But as I watch, I wonder,
If someone is crying,
because living things
are in danger of dying . . .

Mari Alwena Jones (14)
Ysgol Gyfun Ystalyfera

My Cats

My cats sleep
Anywhere
Any table
Any chair
Top of the piano
On the window ledge
In the middle
Or on the edge
In an open drawer
Or even an empty shoe
Anybody's
Lap will do!

Fitted in a
Cardboard box
In a cupboard
or even with
your frocks!
Anywhere!
They don't care!
My cats sleep
Anywhere!

**Owain Bates (12)
Ysgol Gyfun Ystalyfera**

FOOD

I like food there is no doubt,
From jacket potatoes to lemon fried trout.

I like crisps especially Pringles,
You put them in your mouth and they make your tongue tingle.

A plate of chips with vinegar and salt,
When I start eating them I can't halt.

Apples, bananas, pears and grapes,
They make me jump around like a giant ape

Hot buttered toast with a blob of jam,
Is nicer to eat than a sandwich full of Spam.

I like food inside or out but I can't eat a smelly green sprout.

Andrea Bazley (11)
Ysgol Gyfun Ystalyfera

YOU

You were the waves in my deep blue sea,
The sun in my solar system,
The candle in my darkness,
The flower in my tree.

You brought me happiness, love and care,
You fed me when I was hungry,
When I was ill, you cured me,
When I was sad you cheered me.

But now, there is an emptiness inside,
For you have sadly left,
Your heart of gold will shine for eternity,
In the leaves that fell, for ever.

Cadi Dewi (13)
Ysgol Gyfun Ystalyfera

IT'S THE INNOCENT THAT DIE...

Anger, voices raised, guns and bombs in the air,
A motherless child cries for the home, flattened
By an evil, angry, faceless body...
But it's the innocent that die...

Shattered disfigured bodies lie upon the city
pavement,
Blood-stained odour, rubbled ruins of the once
busy centre,
Torn, white faces stare, anxiously, waiting...
But it's the innocent that die...

Clenched angry fists batter, anticipating cries,
A school yard of everlasting torment,
Cold money grasped by hands,
Should this bullied innocent die?

Silently a dwelling door is secretly unclosed,
Shaking hands, eyes lost in senility,
Gasps as sudden panic overcomes her subdued
serenity,
It's always the innocent that die...

Elen Hâf Richards (13)
Ysgol Gyfun Ystalyfera

My Friends And I

My friends and I have a really good laugh
Especially when we're in school
Laura, Gayle, Claire and Michelle
they're all really cool.

We sometimes go shopping
or just out and about
we give each other manicures
and sing and dance and shout.

We always have a good laugh
We're always laughing aloud.
Not often are we down in the dumps
We're always up and loud.

When one is under the weather
we always call and ask
'Is she doing all right now?
Or take chicken soup in a flask.
Whenever we don't get along
We think of what we've done
We miss each other and get together
We stay friends as hard as we can.

Kim Richards (13)
Ysgol Gyfun Ystalyfera

Nightfall

The sun is drowned in the marshes,
A seagull crying at another,
These are the only living things.

Night shadows creep over the ground,
Everybody home safe and sound,
Peace and quiet on the street,
Family's home watching *Coronation Street.*

The sea tide meets the river,
Their waters mingle without a sound,
Nobody about, no creatures either,
Peace and quiet at nightfall.

Bethan Morgan (11)
Ysgol Gyfun Ystalyfera

NOCTURNAL SOUNDS

Everywhere is silent,
I cannot hear a sound,
And as the daylight fades.
Night shadows creep over the ground.

All outside is quiet,
The wind is very slight,
And all the world is ready,
For the mysteries of the night.

Mice play on the road,
There's no danger of a car,
As everybody's sleeping well,
Under the midnight stars.

The owls are all out hunting,
The bats are wide awake,
Everything is reflected,
Silhouetted on the lake.

The moon is now out fully,
After emerging from a cloud,
All the night life's partying,
Now the night seems loud.

Hywel Rees (14)
Ysgol Gyfun Ystalyfera

FIRST MEETING

Golden stone steps browned by July rain
The fountain springs joyfully, cascading down its stairway
And crashes excitedly,
As does my heart.

I stand, a lone figure in a mac
An indigo beacon at the top of Castle Square,
Eyes searching - for his familiar form,
I descend the stairs,
The mac billowing like a bride's train.

Heart pounding I see him
Tall, brown-haired, blue-eyed,
I do not even reach his shoulder
As he takes both my small, silver-ringed hands,
And gently kisses my soaked forehead.

Then stands away
As we take in each other's appearance
Uncaring of the cold rain
In the warmth of our new friendship.

Angharad Carys Thomas (15)
Ysgol Gyfun Ystalyfera

THE SUNFLOWER

Standing tall and proud,
Above all the rest.
As tall as a skyscraper,
Almost touching the sky.

Large disc with yellow rays,
Petals the colour of the sun,
With a golden yellow mane,
Like a fully grown lion.

Fields that stretch for miles,
Full of smiling faces,
Swaying back and forth in the wind,
Dancing with each other.

Fiona Michelle Humphreys (13)
Ysgol Gyfun Ystalyfera

MUDDLED UP MARTIN!

This is the story of Martin
The green man from Mars,
Who came down to Earth
And went visiting bars!

He'd got himself plastered
Was sick and turned gray,
Got lost in his spaceship
Cruising along the Milky Way.

When his martian friends found him
All gray in a spin,
Crash landed in space dust
What a state he was in!

They got him home safely
Then they put him to bed,
When he woke a week later
To his leader he was led.

His captain said 'Martin!'
The aim of our plan,
Was to study Mars chocolate
Not the bar at *The Green Man.*'

Rhian Indeg Snowdon (13)
Ysgol Gyfun Ystalyfera

Woods

Leaves whispering to each other,
Toadstools popping their heads out
Of the ground,
Elves singing and dancing,
Juicy blackberries ripening.

People who come in the summer.
Have picnics under
Huge branches.

Rabbits digging holes
For burrows,
Poisonous snakes,
Like foxes as they hunt.

Enormous trees,
Giants of the forest,
Acorns that grow into oaks,
Lord of the kingdom.

Emily Fyfield (11)
Ysgol Gyfun Ystalyfera

Underwater City

Under the mysterious ocean
Lies a forgotten city
Of sunken ships and wrecks.
The fish explore it freely
And the sharks guard it with pride.

Tropical fish of all shades
like a cloud of colours
cruising slowly as if lost
in this underwater city.

The seaweed dances happily
swaying in the current
as if competing for gold
in the underwater Olympics.

Matthew Maddocks (13)
Ysgol Gyfun Ystalyfera

THE MORNING

Birds are singing,
Cockerels crowing,
Brightness growing,
In the morning.

People waking,
Dawn is breaking,
Sunlight leaking,
In the morning.

Infants laughing,
As they're playing,
Parents talking,
In the morning.

Children sitting,
While they're waiting,
To start thinking,
In the morning.

The bell's ringing,
School is starting,
Children rushing,
In the morning.

David Roland Parker (12)
Ysgol Gyfun Ystalyfera

WHY?

Such happiness you did fill me with,
excitement overwhelmed me too.
Why did you have to give me hope?
If only I'd known what you'd do.

In some ways I wish I'd never met you,
Others that it was all just a dream.
My feelings are impossible to describe,
I don't know whether to shout, cry or scream.

Now everything seems so pointless,
I've finally blown my fuse.
Nothing seems to make me smile,
there's no more heart left to bruise.

So where do I go from here?
Is this one big exaggeration?
Are my feelings really true?
Or is this just an infatuation?

Roxanne Guard (16)
Ysgol Gyfun Ystalyfera

HOUSE OF ECHOES

The house positioned precariously,
dark trees surrounding dancing maliciously,
Crashing shutters squeaky hinges,
Swinging vigorously in the wind.
Shattered tiles scattered around,
baring the attic to the wrath of clouds.
Forks of lightning, slicing the skies,
angry thunder brings tears to your eyes.

Entering to find yourself confronted by darkness,
aim the torch, light and dark caress.
Shadows leaping wall to wall,
down the dusty stairs comes the bouncing ball.
The laugh of a child echoes from ahead,
Staring up at the eyes of the dead.
Screaming in terror, paralysed with fear,
from this place you should have stayed clear.

Craig Robert Fisher (16)
Ysgol Gyfun Ystalyfera

HOLIDAYS

Holidays are always great fun
This year I went to Spain
I loved the sand, sea and the sun
We only had one day of rain.

During the day I swam in the pool
I met a lot of new friends there
It was the best place to keep cool
As it was so hot everywhere.

In the evenings we went for a walk
We would go for a drink and something to eat
We would sit for a while and talk
As there were lots of people to meet.

Holidays always go too fast
Time goes quick when you're having fun
Good things never seem to last
And soon you have to say goodbye to everyone.

Daniel Briggs (12)
Ysgol Gyfun Ystalyfera

FAIRIES

Their enchanted calls
Mesmerising the mind
Hollowing reality
Escaping from the bitterness of life.

Entering a deep blue sea of happiness
Believing what is not
Betraying life
For a world which cannot be.

A harmony of beauty
A melody of love
Escaping reality
In a mind which believes too much.

But love is not what life is
It's meaningful and true
And fairies are where the joy lies
They're inside me and you.

Nia Rhianwen Williams (14)
Ysgol Gyfun Ystalyfera

AS THE SUN SETS

As the sun sets,
And moonlight appears,
I think of all the people in tears.
We try to help but it's no good.
The world would be better if we could,
But so much damage has been done,
We try to do as much as we can,
But the fighting has torn the world apart,
It's also torn every human heart.

As the sun sets,
And the moonlight appears,
All is lost in tears and fears.
The hunger. The pain.
Are people on earth sane?
Don't send men to moons,
Or travel the world in balloons,
Just get rid of the hurt and sorrow,
And try to find a better tomorrow.

As the sun sets
I hope the fighting will cease,
And pray that one day we will have world peace.

Lowri Williams (13)
Ysgol Gyfun Ystalyfera

THE TOWNIES

Outside the *Spar* - they hang in gangs.
With dyed black roots and fake brown tans
There they stand, chips and cans
Saying 'Oi Mush! I'm king of the land!'

Outside the chippy with gel coated hair
Crooked teeth and empty stare
There they stand, pastie in hand
Shouting 'Oi Mush! I'm king of the land!'

Down the clubs they lurk at night
Drinking *Hooch* and *Diamond White*
There they stand - fags in hand
Saying 'Oi Mush! I'm king of the land!'

Kangol, Kappa, Fila, Nike
Lamberts and *Apollo* bike
There they stand, raving fans
Yelling 'Oi Mush! I rule these lands!'

So hope to God you never meet
A gang of townies in the street.
There they stand, knives in hand
Saying 'Oi Mush! Get off my land!'

Gareth Thomas (14)
Ysgol Gyfun Ystalyfera

THE CAT

It lay on the chair
In front of the fire
A ball of black
Asleep.

It lay there still
Didn't move a muscle
Suddenly, got up
He jumped to the floor.

He moved around
So quiet and frail
Out of the room
I began his trail.

Went to the kitchen
Stared at his food
Took a bite
And looked around.

Moved along
Took his foot off the floor
Turned around
He was out of the door.

Catrin Reed (13)
Ysgol Gyfun Ystalyfera

A Dream Come True

As I travelled along the coast
Not very far from Newquay,
I saw a flash of silver
High above the sea.
I looked again and saw the splash
As it landed in the spray,
I knew then that I had seen
A dolphin in Cardigan Bay.
I felt a stab of happiness
As I saw that graceful mammal,
Happily splashing in the waves
Not far out in the channel.
Yet not so many years ago
That clear blue water was dark
As oil poured form a tanker
Along our coastal park.
The sand was ruined, birds were killed
Other creatures suffered too.
But seeing that dolphin leap so high
Was like a dream come true.
Our lovely coastline is now clean
And I hope it stays that way,
So that we can see the dolphins leap
On another day.

Angharad Jones (13)
Ysgol Gyfun Ystalyfera

City's Cry

Beneath the darkened sky
Beyond the whistles of country men
You hear the city's cry.

Cars honking, music thumping
people shouting
and people complaining.

You'd rather hear
children playing in their gardens
mothers chatting
and polite men excusing their pardons.

I can't say that I like it
that would be a lie
but I have to stand it
I'd rather put up with it than die.

If I could be where I wanted
I'd go far away
I wouldn't have the agony
of living with it from day to day.

But

I still remain here
beneath the darkened sky
In the sound of the city's cry.

Roxanne Chinchen (13)
Ysgol Gyfun Ystalyfera

EVERYDAY WONDERS

I sometimes sit and wonder.
about the things in life,
when the sun comes up every morning,
the things that calm my strife.

I listen to the sweet, sweet song
by the birds that sing each dawn,
I wonder what the trees have seen,
from the time that they were born.

I love to see the butterflies,
dancing on the breeze
and see the many flowers
that are visited by the bees.

And when the darkness falls each night,
the moon and stars are there,
And I just choose the brightest star,
to say this special prayer.

'I hope tomorrow will bring back soon,
The things that make me glad,
That I am sharing on this earth,
the wondrous things I have,
to see the many colours
Each breath I take of air,
I love this world I live in,
because I really care.

Stephanie Hawcutt (14)
Ysgol Gyfun Ystalyfera

IF . . .

If I could go across the sea,
There's only one place I would be.
Somewhere warm, where the palm trees sway,
When I think of this my mind goes astray.

To walk along an endless shore,
I could walk on forever more.
There would be a bottomless, turquoise sea,
Where I'd play - all day if I wanted. Just me.

My house would be a rather nice hut,
And I'd feast on the sweet coconut.
I would dive deep beneath the waves,
And explore all the exotic caves.

I'd watch the fish swim in their shining shoal,
Staying alive, that is their goal.
The colours are amazing - they shimmer and shine,
The coral's breathtaking, it stands like a shrine.

As I lie in the red, dying sun,
Reminding myself of all this fun,
I fall asleep as I hum the sweet rhumba beat,
And find myself back in my dreary old street.

If you were in my position, you'd really despair,
You'd be bald after pulling out all your hair.
Do I do this? Oh no! I just fall asleep,
And pretty soon I'm swimming in the ocean deep.

Lydia Davies (14)
Ysgol Gyfun Ystalyfera

MY SECRET PLACE

When I've had a row or
want to be alone,
I like to go to my secret place
which is my own little zone.

I can listen to my music
and maybe sit and think,
But surely someone will disturb me
before I have time to blink.

It is painted yellow as the sun
and blue like the sea,
And when I'm in my secret place
No one is as happy as me.

My secret place is filled with
lots of bright colours,
And a vase in the window contains
my favourite flowers.

And when my friends come over
and walk through this door,
They always have lots of fun
and never want to go.

This place is fun and has
no gloom or doom,
For my secret place is
my bedroom.

Isla Sheree Humphreys (14)
Ysgol Gyfun Ystalyfera

SUPERSTAR!

You see them in the movies,
They drive their fancy cars,
They're always on their mobile phones,
They are the *Superstars!*

They wear designer labels,
They're very glamorous,
But underneath the make up,
They're very much like us.

But are they really happy?
Is that smile a fake?
Do they find their jobs hard work,
Or a piece of cake?

They're always very busy,
No time for this or that,
People asking questions,
For them to answer back.

They're surrounded by the media,
People from magazines,
They ask the same old questions -
'What's going on behind the scenes?'

I wouldn't like to be a *star*,
It's not all it's made out to be,
You get fame and lots of money,
But there is no privacy.

Owain John (14)
Ysgol Gyfun Ystalyfera

WHEN I GROW UP

When I grow up
I want to be
a millionaire
and sail the sea.

I could star in a film
with the famous Tom Cruise
or be an athlete
if I choose.

I could sing in a concert
or write a book,
or model on the catwalk
with a fashionable look.

I would fly to the moon
and back in a day,
all in time to watch
Home and Away.

I could marry a man
that came from Mars.
We'd take our honeymoon
travelling the stars.

I might forecast the weather
or present on TV
but at the end of the day
I will always be me.

Hannah Gange (13)
Ysgol Gyfun Ystalyfera

THE LAST ERRAND

She was the same age as me, maybe younger!
Drowned with life from the nail of her toe
to the peak of her head.
She was innocent-hearted with soul and beauty.
> Her hair always a perfect shape
> Her legs moved with a continuous pattern
> Her face gleaming with love and happiness.

A neighbour had sent her to call for a bottle of milk.
She strolled along the pavement, youth in her hands.
One step . . . Two steps . . .
Life filled with contentment and good humour,
One step . . . Two steps . . .
Euphoric atmosphere dissolving, laughing voices dying
One step . . . Two steps . . .
Black, dungy clouds pushing the light and sky to one side,
One step . . . Two steps . . .
Deserted town, distraught feelings,
One step . . .
Silence!
'It's a girl!'
Voices of critical soldiers.
'Oh my God! Is she all right?'
Worrying tones combining with those fatal voices!
Bloody surroundings in every direction!

Just a bottle of milk which could turn reality into death!
As innocent as a picture on the wall
Or the changing of the weather.

Spilt Milk = *Life at end.*

Katie Grounds (12)
Ysgol Gyfun Ystalyfera

A LAZY AFTERNOON

On a lazy afternoon upon a summer's day,
down the garden path,
the kittens, there they lay
a purring, a mewing, to pass the hours away.

'I'm tired,' said the black cat
'You look it' said the white,
'Did you have a night out
on the tiles last night?'

On a lazy afternoon, upon a summer's day,
down along the garden path,
the kittens, there they lay
a purring, a mewing, to pass the hours away.

'Do you like that dog?' said the black cat
'Not much' said the white
'he leaps out of dark corners,
and gives me such a fright.'

On a lazy afternoon, upon a summer's day,
down along the garden path,
the kittens, there they lay
a purring, a mewing, to pass the hours away.

'I'm hungry,' said the black cat.
'So am I' said the white
'What do you think of that *Whiskas* food?'
'I think it tastes . . . alright.'

On a lazy afternoon, upon a summer's day,
down along the garden path,
the kittens, there they lay
a purring, a mewing, to pass the hours away.

Bethan Wallace (14)
Ysgol Gyfun Ystalyfera

THE ALIEN

In my house there lives an alien,
Its room is next to mine,
It sleeps in a bed like you and I,
And hides there all the time.

It's there when there is work to be done,
And when it's misbehaved,
Or when it doesn't get its way,
It sulks there in its cave.

If you ever dare to step in there
Then you're in for a shock,
It smells, it stinks, it's like a tip,
It should be under lock.

Don't dare look underneath its bed,
God knows what's lurking there,
Perhaps something living or something dead?
Mouldy food - it doesn't care.

It weighs in at around nine stone one,
And stands at five foot four,
Aged approximately twelve years old,
And its IQ's not much more.

It has big brown eyes, a crooked mouth,
And fangs that give a scare,
It's got lanky legs and huge, big feet
And short brown spiky hair.

This alien has another name,
Given by my mother,
Brace yourself, wait for it -
Edward Dennis, he's my brother!

Frances Dennis (14)
Ysgol Gyfun Ystalyfera

WATCHING THE WORLD GO BY

It does not seem that long ago
I was a seed upon the floor.

Now for thousands of years,
here I've stood
In the same old spot
in the same old wood.

I've seen the people come and go
I've seen them laugh and full of woe,
but my friends have gone, my neighbours too,
there was nothing I could do.

Two thousand years ago, it must have been,
when Jesus was right here in this scene.
There were no roads just lanes and paths,
no cars and lorries just horses and carts.

The water was fresh, the air was clean.
There was no pollution to be seen.
But the rain that now falls is no longer sweet,
It burns the grass around my feet,
and now the earth it starts to crack,
the water's musty and the air is black.

The seas around start to boil
as man misuses coal and oil,
My branches wave from north to south
I taste the acid rain within my mouth.
My trunk is strong but not for much longer
as plans for a motorway are getting stronger.

So here I shall watch the world go by
until it's time for me to die.

Rhian Bazley (13)
Ysgol Gyfun Ystalyfera

LIFE . . .

If I fall, will someone miss me?
Will the sounds of crashing waves below
mask my voice from the world?
Will the sea of anger carry my body,
and wash the rocks of my blood-like hate?
Will the rapacious birds feed on my poisoned flesh,
and make me live forever?
I hate to live . . . but I'd hate to die!

Maybe I could be a part of someone's life!
A part of some importance, maybe, then,
maybe not, for what have I to live for?
Am I to become successful - like my forefathers?
Wallow in a pool of hate, or drown in a sea of pity?
I'd hate to die . . . but I'd hate to live!

My life has slipped through my fingers,
like the sands of time.
Dodging the good, but growing from bad,
that is how I've survived.
Now I've nothing to live for,
my money gone, my family left.
It's painful to stay, when no one wants you.
I hate to live . . . but I'd hate to die!

So now I farewell thee, dear world.
To you I owe my existence.
My poverty, my hate, my anger.
I am a disappointment to everyone,
in everything I do.
I'll be the one to end all the pain
in one sudden jerk, I'll put a stop to everything.
I hate to live . . . so now - I must die!

Jessica Wearing Evans (14)
Ysgol Gyfun Ystalyfera